WHOLE CHILD

PARENTING

TODDLER
(12 to 24 Months)

Concept by Claudia Sandor

WHOLE CHILD

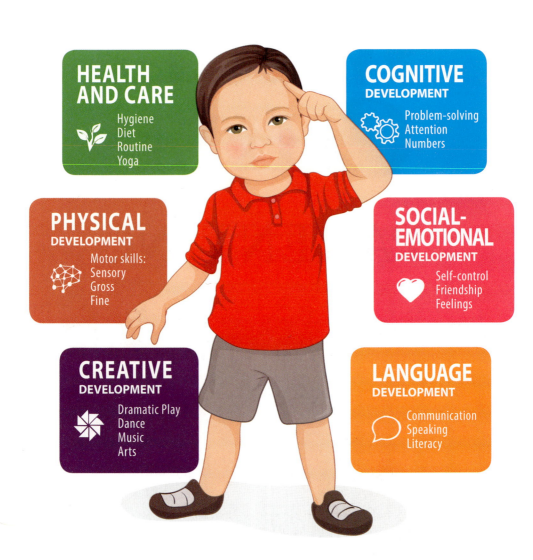

WHOLE CHILD

whole \hōl\ **child** \chi-əld\ *compound noun*
1 : a child who is completely developed in all six areas

A **whole child** grows up to reach his or her full potential.

A **whole child** is a **well-rounded** person and lifelong learner.

A **whole child** is ready to face the world with **confidence.**

A **whole child** has **self-esteem, knowledge,** and **creativity**.

A **whole child** will live a **happy** and **fulfilling life**.

Being a successful parent starts with understanding your child.

The Whole Child Parenting Program covers every aspect of a child's cognitive, social-emotional, language, creative, physical, and health and care development.

By using clear examples, color-coded stages, simple and logical steps, age-appropriate materials and toys, developmentally appropriate activities and workbooks, and core parenting books, the Whole Child Program will change the way you think about learning.

Welcome to parenting for the new millenium!

Copyright © 2016 Whole Child Parenting, Inc.

All rights reserved.
No part of this book may be reproduced or transmitted in any form or by any means, electronic, mechanical, photocopy, recording, digital, or any information storage and retrieval system now known or to be invented, without written permission from the publisher, except by a reviewer who may quote brief, attributed excerpts in connection with a review.

Published by Whole Child Parenting, Inc.
Whole Child Parenting books, activity books, toys, and materials are available at special discounts when purchased in bulk for premiums and sales promotions as well as for fundraising or educational use.
For details, please contact us at:
sales@wholechild.co

Whole Child is a registered trademark of Whole Child, LLC
Library of Congress Control Number: 2016905514
ISBN 978-1-944930-00-4

Created by the Whole Child Education Team with:
Early Childhood Education Specialist, Erin Weekes
Book design by Willabel Tong
Art direction by Dan Marmorstein
Editorial direction by Editorial Services of Los Angeles

Visit us on the web at: www.wholechild.co
Email us at: publishing@wholechild.co

Printed in the United States of America.
1 3 5 7 9 10 8 6 4 2

Contents

Introduction:

What Is Whole Child Parenting? vi

Toddler:

Milestones 2

Chapter 1:

Cognitive Development 4
Attention Span 8
Math and Numbers 12
Spatial Relationships 14
Cause and Effect 16
Problem Solving 18
Symbolic Play 20

Chapter 2:

Social-Emotional Development 22
Social Development 26
Emotional Development 28
Self-Regulation 30
Self-Awareness 34

Chapter 3:

Language Development 36
Listening and Understanding 40
Communication and Speaking, 42
Sign Language

Emergent Literacy 44

Chapter 4:

Creative Development 46
Music 50
Dance 52
Visual Arts 54
Dramatic Play 56

Chapter 5:

Physical Development 58
Gross Motor Skills 62
Fine Motor Skills 64
Sensory Motor Skills 66

Chapter 6:

Health and Care 68
Hygiene, *Hair, Skin, Eyes, Nails,* 70
   Ears, Tooth Care
Diet, *Calories, Allergies, Safety,* 76
   Tummy Troubles
Potty Training 82
Routine, *Two Naps in One* 84
Mind and Body 86
   Aggressive Behavior, Yoga

Reaching Milestones 88
Toddler Environment 90
   Whole Child Room Elements

What Is Whole Child Parenting?

It Is Parenting from Head to Toe

Whole child parenting involves exposing your child to everything he needs to be happy, healthy, well adjusted, smart, and developing right on track. A whole child is a well-rounded person, someone whose innate talents have been developed in every major milestone category and who is ready to face the world with confidence. A whole child has the self-esteem and knowledge to develop his true potential.

Whole child parenting is you doing what you can, with our help, to get him there. **The Whole Child Parenting Program is for busy people just like you.** With interactive materials that support you at every step, using toys, workbooks, activities, videos, web support, and an app, the Whole Child Parenting Program takes into account the whole child and helps you, the parent or primary caregiver, do what is necessary and best for your child at every stage, every age from infancy to five years old. **It helps you parent with a purpose, giving you practical advice and materials** that explain the whys and how-tos and goals of each step you take to help your child grow.

Whole child parenting is a process that begins with you. It can be overwhelming to think about the responsibility you have to your toddler in one of the most important years of his life.

This toddler year is a crucial year because development, in both the body and brain, is happening at a rapid pace. This toddler year will continue to set the stage for how your child problem solves, communicates, socializes, and thinks for

INTRODUCTION

the rest of his life. That is not to say that you won't have amazing experiences with your child when he is 12–24 months old. You will have absolutely transformative experiences with your toddler-age child during these next twelve months. You will get to see life from the perspective of a person who is isn't even three feet tall! And **your presence and influence will always matter the most in these first five years.** The world is constantly changing; will your child be ready for the global economy years from now? Just by reading this book you are setting yourself along the right path for being the best parent you can be for your toddler-age child.

HOW TO GET ON THE RIGHT TRACK NOW

Whole Child Parenting: Toddler has six chapters for the six areas of development seen in the column at right. **Each area of development is assigned its own color.**

Each of the six chapters begins with a chart and summary to introduce you to the concepts and terminology in the pages ahead. Within each chapter, **you will also get real-life activities and insights that paint a picture of how your child demonstrates these developmental concepts** in everyday life. In addition to examples, there are tips and advice for parents and primary caregivers to use to support and guide you as you and your child encounter and master each of the upcoming milestones.

The Whole Child Parenting Program has developed five smart, modern, easy steps to help you raise a happy, thriving child.

1 Cognitive Development

2 Social-Emotional Development

3 Language Development

4 Creative Development

5 Physical Development

6 Health and Care

> The Whole Child Parenting Program involves:
>
> 1. Committing yourself
> 2. Educating yourself
> 3. Creating the right environment
> 4. Using the right materials
> 5. Staying on track

That's it. Five steps to making your experience with your child the most rewarding and productive experience in your life.

STEP ONE: COMMITTING YOURSELF

Let's start with commitment. As a parent you have already taken the huge step of accepting responsibility for the little person in front of you. What is next required might not even be a step that needs articulating for you, but it bears repeating here: **You need to commit quality time to raising your whole child.**

There is no formula or script when it comes to being successful in parenting. Many parents look to doctors, textbooks, and experts for the secrets to parenting success. And while all of these are great sources, none address the whole child. And the whole child needs your attention.

Each child is different and has a different temperament, different interests, and a different personality. As a parent, you are also different. Every parent has different values that come from being a part of different cultures, socioeconomic classes, education levels, religions, and family sizes. The best way to be successful in parenting is to be involved with your child. By being involved and communicating with your child, you are better able to support her and her needs.

Many wonder what the real measures and outcomes of good parenting are. It does not involve your child having a high IQ, being talented in sports, or making a lot of money. Good parenting results in raising a child who grows up to give back to society, is independent, has a good work ethic, gets along well with others, and understands her identity and self-worth.

When it comes to measuring your success as a parent, it is important to look at the quality of the relationship you have with your child and not how effectively you can control your child. Just because your child listens and follows the rules does not mean she understands or respects them; it just means she is obedient.

The quality of your relationship has to do with your involvement and communication with your child. Know what guidelines are appropriate to set for your child, and explain them in a way that shows why these rules are necessary and important. As a parent, you need to meet your child's needs and help her feel respected. This can be done by explaining the reasons behind rules and discussing your child's feelings and opinions.

When your child feels like she is a valued member of the family and the community, she will then develop the confidence needed to begin moving toward being independent and making her own decisions.

Parents who are uninvolved with their children tend to make their children feel ignored and unvalued. At the same time, parents who are overly controlling and establish strict rules over all avenues of their children's lives tend to make their children feel stressed and have low self-esteem. It is important to find the middle ground between controlling your child and overlooking your child.

Your child is born naturally impulsive, immature, and ambitious, and she looks to you for guidance and support. This is why it is important to **make sure you communicate clear guidelines and expectations** for your child to alleviate stress and misunderstandings.

THE FOUR STYLES OF PARENTING

Whole Child Parenting: Toddler combines research, expert advice, and firsthand experience. In the past few decades, early childhood education has grown exponentially.

In the late 1950s, psychologist Erik Erikson organized development from birth to death into eight stages; according to Erikson, a person cannot successfully excel in the next stage of life without first completing the stage before.

Looking specifically at the first three stages, which cover ages birth to five, we see that a person's success lies first in his relationship with his parents. **Stage 1,** covering ages birth to two years old, focuses on a child's ability to develop **trust** with his parents. From there, children move on to **Stage 2** (for ages two to four years old), when the child is developing autonomy. **Autonomy** is your child's sense of self as an individual. Your child develops a sense of self by exploring the environment, learning about his own interests, and testing his limits. Moving forward to **Stage 3** (ages four to five years old), your child is **finding his purpose and place** within the family.

In the last 40 years, developmental psychologists have established **four styles of parenting.** The best parenting style is a combination of these four parenting styles—one in which you approach different situations with different solutions and always communicate with your child.

Authoritarian Parenting

The authoritarian parenting style can best be described as strict. Authoritarian parents tend to set rules that result in rewards or punishment if they are not followed. Rules are not explained and usually follow a reasoning of "because I said so." **These parents usually set high demands and expect obedience** but are not very responsive to their children. Children who grow up under the authoritarian parenting style tend to be obedient and usually well performing in school but socially exhibit signs of shame, low self-esteem, and lowered happiness levels.

Authoritative Parenting

The authoritative parenting style establishes rules and guidelines for children instead of just demands. Authoritative parents are more nurturing and forgiving, rather than simply punishing. They are responsive to their children and willing to listen and answer questions.

An important quality of authoritative parents is that they create clear standards for their children and adjust those standards based on their children's conduct.

Children who grow up under the authoritative parenting style tend to be capable and successful at learning new things. Socially and emotionally, they feel accepted and tend to be happy.

Permissive Parenting

The permissive parenting style is one that has few demands or guidelines. Parents tend to have low expectations for their children's maturity and abilities. **Permissive parents are more lenient with rules, preferring to avoid confrontation. This parenting style is usually nurturing and communicative but leaves children looking at their parent as more of a friend.** Children who grow up under the permissive parenting style tend to often have poor self-regulation skills and may experience problems with authority and have trouble in school.

Uninvolved Parenting

The uninvolved parenting style is one with even fewer demands as well as little communication and responsiveness. Uninvolved parents fulfill their children's basic needs but tend to be detached and unavailable for their children in all other areas. **Children who grow up under the uninvolved parenting style tend to have low self-esteem,** a hard time regulating their emotions, and a hard time making friends.

Your child's personality and temperament play a major role in how you choose your parenting style. Research shows correlations between parenting styles and their impact on children. There is also evidence showing other factors, such as a child's personality and the outside environment, playing a role as well. Your larger environment—such as culture, religion, socioeconomic class, and family style—can also affect how your child reacts to your parenting. School, friends, and personality play a significant role in how your child responds to your parenting style.

It is important to be consistent with your parenting style, especially when it comes to discipline and setting expectations for your child. Besides taking into account her environment, think about other people in your child's life, such as your spouse or partner or caregiver. Take time to talk to each other about parenting styles and how you will work together when raising your child. Talk about what you both value as important and how you were each raised; this is important for keeping your parenting style consistent.

At the end of the day, you need to remember to be present and realistic. **Be present both physically and mentally in order to be responsive to your child's needs.** Be realistic in your expectations and the guidelines you set for your child.

Committing quality time as a parent, whichever parenting style(s) you choose, is the single most important factor in your child's healthy development.

STEP TWO: EDUCATING YOURSELF

Addressing the whole child means knowing about the general developmental milestones your child will experience at each age. Milestones define peak stages of accomplishment when your child achieves the end of one stage before moving on to the next. **Milestones are exciting, because when a child reaches one you get to see how far she has come.** And you get to look forward to the next amazing stage your whole child will go through.

But how can you be aware of milestones without knowing the specific developmental categories the stages occur in? How can you have realistic expectations about what is age appropriate and what your whole child should or should not be doing? *Whole Child Parenting: Toddler* **lays out six major developmental areas of your child's growth and follows them through this year of your child's development.**

Cognitive development

The first area of development is cognitive development. Cognitive development refers to the process of learning and the growth of intelligence and other mental capabilities, such as memory, reasoning, problem solving, and thinking. Memory and problem solving play a large role in your child's ability to engage in science, mathematical thinking, and logic.

Your involvement strengthens your child's cognitive abilities over these next years and plays a significant role in her school readiness and how she will learn and retain information later in life. At birth, your child's brain is only a quarter of the size of an adult brain; by age five, it has grown to be close to the same size and volume as yours.

Take advantage of these first five years to set the path and exercise the brain to its fullest potential. The Whole Child Parenting Program will very clearly define the stages of cognitive development and will help you be involved in your child's growth in this area.

Social-emotional development

Social-emotional skills reflect how effectively your child is able to interact in social settings. In order to interact well he must develop positive relationships. He must learn to recognize and regulate his emotions and reactions while communicating his feelings.

For young children, social-emotional skills provide a pivotal foundation upon which are built a range of other skills that are necessary in preschool as well as on play dates. Development in this category will help to determine how well your child succeeds with peer interaction throughout his life.

In order to interact well with others your child must develop positive relationships with others. He must also effectively coordinate his actions with communicating his feelings. As well, he must learn to recognize and regulate his emotions and reactions in many different social settings.

Your child needs to have good self-regulatory skills (i.e. the ability to calm himself down), keen emotional understanding (i.e. learning with help what made him feel the way he does), and growing communication skills such as naming how he feels and dealing with those feelings.

Language development
Language development is how your child communicates, from basic sounds and gestures to the use of pictures in books and words for speaking. As she ages your child will be communicating more than her emotions and needs. She will begin to tell stories, ask questions, and describe people and objects.

Your child will use memory to remember words and past events when telling stories. At an early age, your child's memory will also play a role in symbolic play when she uses props and objects as symbols to represent her ideas. These symbols will later translate to letter recognition and emerging literacy.

The Whole Child Parenting Program identifies how to use sign language to support early literacy skills, and we also include signs in supplemental and supportive materials in the program. Sign language for communication plays a role in your child's social-emotional development because it makes her better able to convey her emotions and needs when she is largely preverbal.

Creative development
Creative development involves how your child uses music, art, movement, and dramatic play to express himself and build imaginative thinking. When doing art, let your child make a mess and indulge in all the different textures and materials you provide. Make a paintbrush or other tools available to your child and then let him explore the paint with his hands. **Creative development plays a big role in your child's physical development as well.** Music and movement build your child's gross motor skills (big muscles) by allowing your child to test balance and large body movements. Visual art builds your child's fine motor skills (small muscles) by allowing him to explore materials such as scissors, paintbrushes, and crayons.

Creative development can be used as an avenue for social-emotional development. Through art and dramatic play, your child can express and act out feelings, model behavior, or work through emotions.

Through activities, examples, and tips, *Whole Child Parenting: Toddler* shows how important creative development can be to your child's other areas of development as well.

Physical development

Physical development refers to your child's control over fine motor skills (small muscle movements of fingers, toes, and wrists) and gross motor skills (bigger movements that use the large muscles in the arms, legs, and torso). Between birth and five years old, your child's body and motor abilities make great strides.

Physical development has a lot to do with your child's self-esteem and sense of trust. Your child is more willing to test her physical skills of throwing, kicking, and balancing when she feels comfortable and confident within her environment.

Physical development is important because it plays a large role in children developing independence and self-help skills. Getting dressed, feeding themselves, and cleaning up are all skills that involve both fine and gross motor skills, which, when combined, develop sensory motor skills.

The Whole Child Parenting Program explains how your child's physical changes correlate with the development of motor abilities and overall physical growth and development.

Health and care

This section discusses safety, grooming, self-help, and the health of your child. As your child grows older, he will be more independent with his hygiene, from small achievements like brushing his own teeth to bigger accomplishments like potty training.

As he goes through each developmental stage, your child's body is changing and growing at a swift pace. He is growing taller, sprouting new teeth, and becoming more active, which will reflect in changes in his diet each year.

Whole child parenting also involves using yoga. Yoga is a great resource in which to engage your child from infancy through age four and beyond. Not only does it allow your child to explore his balance, but it also strengthens his social-emotional development by helping him find an avenue to calm himself. Yoga can also provide a bonding experience for parent and child.

Reaching Milestones

An important and exciting addition to our exploration of the six developmental categories is the Reaching Milestones section we provide at the end of the book. This assessment list will allow you to see everything your child should be doing and accomplishing developmentally around that age. Milestone assessments provide an exciting reflection of all that you are doing to support your whole child.

STEP THREE: CREATING THE RIGHT ENVIRONMENT

Now that you have committed your time and started educating yourself, it is time to follow through by setting up the right environment. Setting up an environment where your whole child will thrive plays a large role in all six areas of their development.

The importance of play

We are in a day and age in which there is an abundance of technology and information available to us. It is hard to remember a time when an answer to a question wasn't a mouse click away or we couldn't watch a video about how to fix something.

Technology has made our lives so much easier over the years, but that is not the case when it comes to our little ones. **Young children need to have the opportunity to make their own connections and discoveries within their environment.** Children between the ages of birth and three learn the most through play.

When setting up an environment that fosters **free play**, it is important to have child-sized furniture as well as incorporate baskets and trays for storing toys. Child-sized furniture and organizational materials such as bins and trays for different categories of toys help your child build independence and self-help skills. Being able to pick what he wants to play with from the shelf or bin will build upon your child's personal interests.

Just because your child is more in control of what activity and materials he is exploring in free play does not mean that you do not need to be involved in free play with your child. Setting up learning and play environments and making learning materials available is just part of encouraging free play. When watching your child explore materials in free play, it is important to interact with him.

The main aspect to remember about free play is that your child's interests guide it.

Structured play is also an important type of play and can help foster and build specific skills. Structured play differs from free play based on the fact that you are planning the activity and materials in which your child is engaging. You are leading the way with a specific activity that has a specific goal. Examples of structured activities can be doing a science experiment with your child or sorting different colored blocks. It is important to have both a combination of structured and free play activities available for your child.

Indoor environments

Incorporating child-sized furniture as well as baskets and trays for storing toys helps your child build independence and self-help skills.

Trays and baskets allow you to provide more manipulatives (age appropriate toys that foster growth) for your child and make it easier for your child to help care for and clean her environment. **When furniture and materials are at your child's eye level, she is able to have better control of her physical movements and be more aware of her environment.**

When setting up an environment that is beneficial for your child's language skills, it is important to have age-appropriate books available. Your child's interest in books both while reading with you as well as pretending to read on her own helps her relate words to pictures. Take your child's language learning to the next level and place labels like TABLE on your kitchen table. Your child will start making the connection between words and objects.

When doing art, let your child get messy and indulge in all the different textures and materials you provide. Investing in an easel, putting down a tarp, providing a smock, or buying washable paint can help you make your indoor environment fit for creative exploration. Having some paper and crayons out on a table that is child-sized makes expressing herself and her ideas easy. She can use the crayons to express herself creatively and create symbols that depict her feelings or needs.

Besides art materials, your child can express her thoughts and feelings through dramatic play by modeling roles and situations when dressing up or using props. Having a mirror in your child's room allows her to explore her self-concept skills. You will find your child making different faces in the mirror or watching herself stack blocks. Having a mirror that is at your child's eye level builds her self-concept by developing a better understanding of herself as an individual who has her own interests and ideas. Don't overwhelm your child with too many choices or structured activities, but instead follow your child's needs and interests to help encourage independence.

Your commitment to your child is very important when it comes to building attention span and memory skills. Having a rug or a chair that is child-sized will make your child more comfortable and thus want to spend longer on an activity. Your child's attention span is a cognitive skill, and it grows as your child grows older.

INTRODUCTION

The Whole Child Parenting Program provides you with all the guidelines, furniture, educational books, activities, supplies, and toys for your whole child's stimulating environment.

Outdoor environments

Environments where your child can engage in free play allow him to develop self-identity and develop his own interests. He is able to learn more about himself by testing his cognitive and physical limits. There aren't always many opportunities for your child to fully engage in free play at home, which is why **outdoor environments provide beneficial play spaces for your child.**

By its nature, play is flexible, changeable, and multifaceted, so your child's play environment should reflect those criteria as well. Play is a core and vital component of how young children learn. Structured and unstructured play provide health benefits by allowing your child to be physically active as well as engaging in problem-solving and creative exploration.

Outdoor environments provide space and opportunities for structured activities that help children learn to communicate and work together, while unstructured activities in large, open areas help your child push limits and take risks.

Your child can make a mess, climb, shout, jump, and run as fast as he wants in open spaces. He can fully express himself and explore his body's movements. From this, your child will develop a sense of competence and confidence in his own physical abilities.

Large, open areas provide opportunities for your child to be creative and use his imagination. He can make connections and witness vivid colors, patterns, and textures in an outdoor environment.

Without material items, media, or structured rules, children can create their own games, engage in dramatic play, and entertain themselves through the use of their mighty imagination.

Nature provides an abundance of science and math opportunities that your child can explore and manipulate. Problem solving, learning cause and effect, and investigating use all of your child's senses. Your child will be exposed to nature and its elements and make connections by witnessing weather, ecology, growth, and natural life cycles. He can explore what happens when he throws a rock in a pond, adds water to dirt or sand, or watches snow melt.

It is not always easy to find a safe outdoor environment for your child. For families in the city, it may mean you need to travel a little farther, but the benefits are worth it. Outdoor environments can actually be considered cleaner than indoor environments, especially when it comes to germs.

By being in a large space with richly fresh air, germs and infectious agents are spread out. Indoor spaces tend to be more enclosed, which leaves bacteria to sit on surfaces and linger. Overall, the benefits of outdoor environments are enormous, and you need to take advantage of them.

How you set up your child's indoor and outdoor environments plays a large role in how he learns and develops. It is important to remember that you are a part of his environment and **in order for your child to thrive, he needs both a rich learning environment and your involvement.**

STEP FOUR: USING THE RIGHT MATERIALS

As parents, we frequently buy and invest in products and toys that are not age appropriate and serve no purpose developmentally, which is why the Whole Child Parenting Program has created developmentally appropriate tools and materials for the whole child that are both fun and educational.

When starting the Whole Child Parenting Program from infancy, you are able to build and adjust your child's environment and learning materials as she grows older. Many materials, such as toys and furniture, are able to grow with your child from infancy to kindergarten. Other materials, such as Whole Child Parenting activity books, toys, and parent resources, assist you with staying on track with your child's development while also helping you plan and measure your time and commitment to your child. The Whole Child Parenting Program is here to walk with you through these first five years.

A variety and quantity of materials are needed to accommodate young children's short attention spans. Children learn through concrete activities, and parents must be able to provide activities for both their physical, active needs and calm, quiet needs.

Having the right environment with both active and quiet play can help your child's social-emotional development by encouraging self-regulating skills. Having a quiet area to go to when your child feels overstimulated or needs a break is just as essential as having a safe area for her to be active and test her physical and creative limits.

A variety of materials is required

to stimulate the development of each age group. Some materials may fit into one or more categories; for example, an art activity can also serve as a fine motor exercise, and dramatic play can also act as a social-emotional tool.

It is important to remember that in order for your child to be able to explore and manipulate materials, she needs to have the materials made easily available to her at all times of the day. Setting up the right environment and investing in furniture that is both safe and easily accessible will play an important role in supporting your child's development.

STEP FIVE: STAYING ON TRACK

Once you have set up your environment, the Whole Child Parenting Program makes staying on track easier by providing you with activity books, toys, and learning materials. **Consistency and routine play a big role in your whole child's development,** so it is up to you to follow through and use these materials with your child.

Five years may seem far away, but time always has a way of sneaking up on us. In the blink of an eye, your child will be five years old and boarding the bus for school. This is a big milestone in your child's life, but you will be confident your child is ready for school because the Whole Child Parenting Program has helped you stay on track with your child's development. Your child is leaving for school a confident, happy, healthy learner.

In the end, all we want for our children is for them to be happy and confident because happiness and confidence set your child on the road to success. The Whole Child Parenting Program is here to get you to that point so you can take a deep breath and know your child is ready to face the world.

Through our *Whole Child Parenting: Toddler* book, educational materials, and workbooks, tips, and activities, apps, videos, and web support, you will have the tools to build a relationship with your child that allows him to confidently express himself through his creative and social-emotional skills, which in turn help him build his cognitive, language, and physical skills. You want your child to be healthy, happy, and complete, developing at or ahead of the curve. The Whole Child Parenting Program was developed for you, the committed and caring parent.

toddler >
(12 to 24 Months)

Milestones for a Toddler

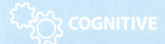 COGNITIVE — 1
- Begins to sort shapes and colors
- Matches pictures with objects
- Recognizes quantities of one to three

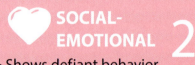 SOCIAL-EMOTIONAL — 2
- Shows defiant behavior
- Shows separation anxiety
- Recognizes themselves in mirror

LANGUAGE — 3
- Says between 10 to 20 words
- Uses two-word sentences
- Follows one-step instructions

 CREATIVE — 4
- Can sing
- Explores art materials
- Dances to music

PHYSICAL — 5
- Runs with ease
- Rides a tricycle
- Holds markers and crayons

 HEALTH AND CARE — 6
- Walks alone
- Uses cup and spoon
- Changes from two naps to one

toddler
(12 to 24 Months)

Between the ages of 12 to 24 months your child is embarking on some new milestones and going through very visible changes. You will see your toddler's arms and legs are becoming stronger, which makes it easier for him to pull himself up to stand and move around. He is able to reach and explore more of his environment. However, with emotions at a high, this can cause some challenging behaviors and tantrums when he does not get what he wants. In this year we will help you with some tips to work with your child and his often challenging (but interesting!) behavior.

1. Cognitive Development

> **Cognitive development refers to how your child's mind is working and his process of learning.**

Cognitive development also involves your child using his senses as well as his motor skills to learn and discover the world around him. Your toddler learns information by engaging in everyday routine activities such as playing, eating, taking trips, and getting dressed.

Your child is using the senses of touch and sight to interact with objects and make connections.

The following chart provides you with an image that walks you through the stages of your child's intellectual development. → *Understanding these areas of cognitive development will help you learn how your child thinks, how to support learning, and how to teach new skills.* →

CHAPTER ONE > COGNITIVE DEVELOPMENT

WHOLE CHILD: TODDLER
Cognitive Development Components

Under each cognitive area, the chart below gives you specific skills you can expect to see as your toddler develops. This chart will allow you to have practical expectations for your child at this age.

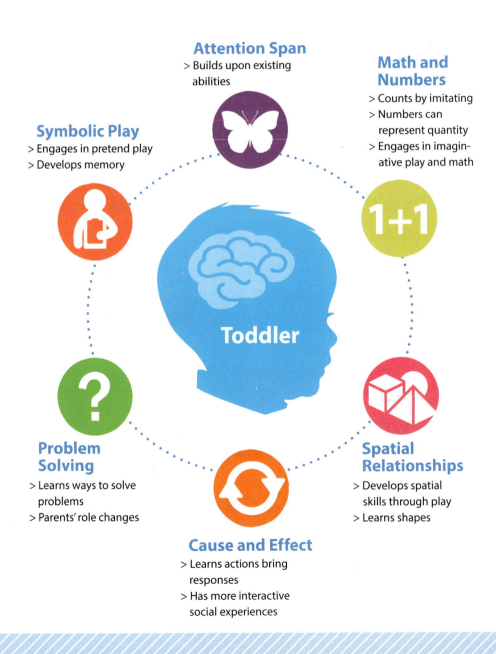

TODDLER > COGNITIVE DEVELOPMENT

Your toddler has the ability to remember an experience that happened some hours prior, or even a day ago. This is demonstrated by watching your toddler repeat a prior experience he had. Take, for example, your child stacking one block on top of the other or using a toy as a phone and talking. Because his brain is expanding, your toddler is able to think in a more complex manner and is beginning to understand symbols during play by realizing those words can represent an object.

Perceptual cognition is a characteristic of cognitive development that enables your toddler to make sense of and understand all of the sensory information he is taking in. Toddlers engage in their world through their senses and learn more about what they taste, touch, smell, hear, and see.

This is why it is very important to allow your toddler to interact in a brain-boosting environment, enabling him to interact with everything around him. Making sure his environment is stimulating and age appropriate will be covered at the end of this chapter.

The subsequent chapters show you how your child acquires knowledge and demonstrates major development in brain growth.

Attention Span >
Concentration

Attention span involves your child being able to focus on an activity or learning experience for an average length of time consisting of two to six minutes.

While it is hard to gather a child's sustained attention at this age, your child will be able to pay attention in a structured activity lead by you. Make sure there are no verbal or visual interferences in your play space, and if your child gets restless, it's time to move on to some other activity.

ACTIVITY

It is a beautiful sunny day, and Jack's parents want to take him to the zoo to see the new giraffe exhibit and watch feeding time. Jack is very excited, so off to the zoo they go!

Upon arriving at the zoo, Jack wants to go straight to see the giraffes. Jack says, "Hurry, Mommy!"

At the exhibit, Jack points to the baby and mommy giraffes and then walks back and forth between the left and right side of the exhibit to see the other giraffes that are standing under the trees.

After a few minutes Jack decides it is time to go and begins to pull on his dad's hand to see a different animal.

Jack's parents are very surprised that he wants to go so soon and before watching feeding time. They are also surprised to see Jack lose interest in the giraffes so quickly.

INSIGHT

In this example, Jack's parents think he has quickly lost his attention regarding the giraffes; however, for his age, Jack has stayed just the right amount of time.

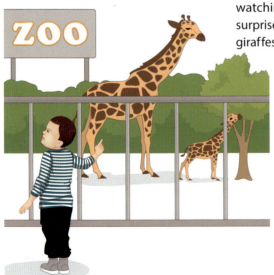

TODDLER > COGNITIVE DEVELOPMENT

Attention skills enable your child to observe, take in information, and learn. Focused attention increases memory, and this supports cognitive development.

This area of cognitive development is getting stronger every day as your child moves closer to two years of age. You will see your little one grow a great deal during the toddler years. **It is important to understand that the change in your child's attention span will not occur overnight.**

When your child was an infant, his attention span was only a few seconds at most. Now that he is a toddler, your child's attention span has expanded and lengthened. This now enables him to do more activities and engage in learning experiences for longer periods of time, thus maximizing learning potential; however, for a parent, the attention span will still feel very short.

An excellent way to build your child's attention span is to teach a new skill a little bit at a time.

Think back to the zoo experience with Jack. Imagine that this time the family visits the giraffes for a brief period. While at the giraffe exhibit Jack mentions that he sees a mommy and a baby giraffe and wants to move on to see something else. Next time when the family visits the zoo, they can extend the time and talk about how the mommy giraffe is bigger than the baby giraffe. By actively building on the experience, Jack's attention span will be extended, giving the opportunity for a new learning experience to take place.

Also, remember to **have clear expectations and consider your child's emotional state before engaging in a learning activity that requires attention.** Your child will be able to better focus if he is not tired or upset or hungry. With these things in mind, you can create a supportive environment for your child to learn.

Some ways that you can support focused attention include:

* Have your child repeat words after you. For example, when you say *giraffe*, *baby*, *mommy*, or *zoo*, have your child repeat the word. This will let you know how much attention your child pays to the conversation or activity.
* Read books with your child and point to pictures. Ask your child to look for certain pictures on the page.

Memory

As your child grows older, he will be able to retain information for longer periods of time.

Your child has the capacity to remember familiar faces, songs, words (*more*, *please*, *Mommy*, *Daddy*, *eat*, and other words that relate to his everyday world), and objects (e.g. pictures or toys) in his environment.

You will hear your child say the word *cat* when he sees one on an afternoon walk, or you will hear him sing the entire song of "Itsy Bitsy Spider" because he remembers all the words.

During memory development, your child is using what is called "working memory," which is your child's ability to keep immediate information in his mind to complete a task. You can see this when you give your toddler verbal instructions such as asking him to get his blanket and take it to his bed, an activity he has participated in time and again. You will also see working memory when your toddler can participate in routines and imitate an action or activity previously observed.

At times, you will notice that your toddler may not remember something. This is perfectly normal since your toddler has not completely mastered the ability to access all the information that is in his memory bank. As your toddler has more practice talking about and piecing together all the experiences he has in a day, his ability to remember and tell you things will increase. **Keeping predictable routines for your child supports his memory development.**

ACTIVITY

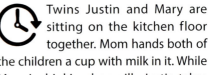Twins Justin and Mary are sitting on the kitchen floor together. Mom hands both of the children a cup with milk in it. While Mary is drinking her milk, Justin takes Mary's cup from her hand and tries to pour his milk into her cup.

Mary starts to cry because she now has milk all over her red shorts.

INSIGHT

Justin remembers seeing his mom pour milk into a cup for him and Mary, and he is trying to do the same thing. Justin is imitating an action that he has observed.

TODDLER > COGNITIVE DEVELOPMENT   11

Each time toddlers practice basic skills, they are drawing from memory. Everyday experiences around the home develop children's cognitive skills.

Remember, the Whole Child Parenting Program offers appropriate developmental products and monthly activity books that walk you through supporting your child's skills. Using these in conjunction with the recommended age-appropriate room materials ensures faster development.

Math and Numbers >
Sense and Awareness

Math and number awareness are the foundations for learning more advanced math concepts.

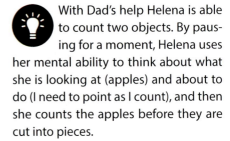

Count how many apples we have.

ACTIVITY

Helena has just come home with Dad from a parent's day out activity. Helena says, "Daddy, I want apple." Dad begins to prepare an afternoon snack for her by getting two apples from the fruit bowl and washing them.

Dad says, "Let's count how many apples we have." Helena looks at the apples for a moment and together they begin to point and count each apple, "One, two . . ."

Then Dad cuts one apple in half and says, "Let's count how many pieces we have. One, two . . ."

Dad then says, "Good job! We have two pieces."

INSIGHT

With Dad's help Helena is able to count two objects. By pausing for a moment, Helena uses her mental ability to think about what she is looking at (apples) and about to do (I need to point as I count), and then she counts the apples before they are cut into pieces.

Math and **number awareness** involves your child recognizing numbers, counting, learning one-to-one correspondence, recognizing patterns, sorting, and classifying.

TODDLER > COGNITIVE DEVELOPMENT

Number sense is seeing how numbers represent an amount. For example, how the symbol "2" is related to a quantity: two apples.

Number sense develops in stages. The first stage occurs during your child's toddler year when you must support your child by helping her learn to count objects out loud and assign each object a number. By assigning each object a number, you are helping your child see that there is a connection between the number and the amount of objects you are counting. As toddlers become older, they will also start to use relational words to indicate *more* or *same* in addition to number words.

During the toddler years, you and your child will count together because your child cannot yet count on her own and extra support is needed; however, as your child reaches the age of two, she will begin to count out loud independently from you. Counting is a huge milestone for your child, and it demonstrates that she understands the concept of number sense.

To support your child's number sense ability, count objects out loud that your child sees in her environment. Objects can include counting out loud how many blocks are on the floor or how many shoes are at the front door.

Just like in the example in which Dad is helping Helena count the pieces of apple for snack, you can also help develop your child's number sense through everyday routines (e.g. counting the number of cups at the table for dinner). By doing so, you are ensuring that your child will be able to succeed in early math and beyond.

Spatial Relationships >
Concepts

Spatial relationships are the relationships between the locations of objects to each other in a given space. This also includes the relationship between your child's own location and objects in a given space.

Spatial relationships can be explained using puzzles. For example, your child is working on a four-piece chunky shaped puzzle, and in order for the puzzle to fit together your child has to move around one puzzle piece to see how it fits next to another. Your child is moving the piece and changing its location within the given space that is the puzzle board. Your child will use trial and error to discover how things move and fit.

Toddlers learn about spatial relationships in a variety of ways, such as by spending time exploring toys in their environment. When playing with a ball, your child will see how the ball can roll into places that are small and that may make it difficult for her to reach with her hands. This is your child learning the relationship between her, an object (the ball), and the space around her.

There are so many simple things you can do to support your child's spatial development, such as giving her a ball to explore. **As your baby plays with her blocks or watches you roll a ball to her, she is learning about spatial relationships.** You can also ask your child to point to her nose, and then follow up by saying, "Your nose is on your face," and "Your nose is on the front of your head," and "Your nose is above your lips." Using words like *on* and *above* supports your child's use of spatial language. Some other examples of spatial language words you can use are *under*, *over*, *on top*, and *next to*.

TODDLER > COGNITIVE DEVELOPMENT

For example, give your child opportunities to climb and jump so she'll learn how she can move up and down stairs. Set up an obstacle course using sheets and pillows; this will allow her to go *over*, *under*, *around*, and *through* different objects, and help her label how she is moving. Say, "You went under the table, and now you are going around the chair."

As your child continues to develop language skills, make sure to use spatial language words as part of your daily routine. **Supporting your child's understanding of spatial relationships will help your child be successful in a number of areas such as reading and math,** as well as aid her in following directions.

ACTIVITY

Simone is playing ball in the living room, and she accidently kicks the ball across the room into the kitchen. The ball rolls under the kitchen chair. Simone runs over to the chair, stops, and then looks at the ball. She reaches her hand out to try and get the ball, but she cannot reach it.

Simone then realizes that in order to get to the ball she will need to bend down and crawl under the chair. As Simone bends down and begins to crawl she still does not feel confident that she will be able to crawl under the chair and reach the ball, so she stands up, pushes the chair over, and then bends down again on the floor.

On this second try, Simone is now able to reach the ball because she has moved an obstructing object in the space and can now access the object she seeks.

INSIGHT

When Simone stops to think, this demonstrates that she is using her problem-solving skills to help her understand the spatial relationship between her size and her ability to reach the ball (object) under the chair.

Cause and Effect >
Actions and Responses

Cause and effect is the relationship between an action and its outcome.

When your child presses a button on a toy and hears it go "beep, beep," he is engaging in cause and effect. The cause is your child pressing the button, and the effect is the sound the toy makes.

Through developing an understanding of cause and effect, your child will build his abilities to solve problems, to make predictions, and to understand the impact of his actions.

The concept of cause and effect is understood further as your child learns that certain actions bring a predictable response. He pushes the toy off the table, and you pick it up for him and place it back on the table. He pushes the toy off the table again. This exchange of cause (pushing the toy off the table) and effect (you pick up the toy) can go on and on to the endless delight of your toddler.

When your child is around 20 months old, you will notice how he experiments with cause and effect when playing with blocks. You will see your child stack one block on top of the other; as he places a third block (cause) on top of the tower, the tower falls down (effect). You will see your toddler try to place a large block on top of a small block (cause). When the large block falls over (effect), it will take your child a few tries before he realizes the small block should go on top.

However, when your child plays with blocks again, he will not remember exactly how the blocks stacked together and will begin to experiment with cause and effect all over again. This is because his memory skills are still developing. **Give him time. These skills develop with age.**

TODDLER > COGNITIVE DEVELOPMENT

ACTIVITY

Twins Catherine and Ian are excited because they are going to music class today. As the twins arrive at music class, the music teacher asks them to come sit on the floor.

The music teacher says, "Hello, everybody! Today you are going to play music with me using a pot and a spoon. This is a pot, and this is a spoon." She holds up each item to the class. "When I start to sing and play my guitar, you can start hitting your pot with the spoon. When I stop singing and playing my guitar, you should stop hitting your pot with the spoon. Watch and listen to me as I show you how."

Then she gives both children a different size pot and a wooden spoon. As she starts to play her guitar and sing, the twins begin to hit their pot with their spoon.

Catherine and Ian start by hitting the pot quietly and then each one gets louder and louder, hitting as hard as they can. The children get so loud they do not hear the teacher stop singing and playing her guitar. The music teacher has to remind the twins to stop.

INSIGHT

Even though Catherine and Ian do not stop hitting on the pot, each child is able to hear that by hitting on the pot they can make a noise. The harder each child hits the pot, the louder the noise gets. The causative action is hitting the pot with the spoon, and the effect is the noise it makes.

Problem Solving >
Thinking Skills

Problem solving is how your child comes up with solutions to complex challenges.

Your child may stand on a chair (solution) to reach a toy on the shelf (challenge).
  Toddlers solve problems by various means: manipulating objects, imitating solutions found by others, using objects as tools, and participating in trial and error.

ACTIVITY

 Sixteen-month-old Lance is in his bedroom playing with his toy fire truck. He knows that his toy fire truck makes a sound, but he can't remember what he has to do to hear it.

Lance starts to shake the toy fire truck, turn it upside down, push the lights on the front, and even pull out the ladder trying hard to make the fire truck make a noise.

Finally, he presses the red circle (siren) button at the top of the truck and the fire truck makes a noise!

INSIGHT

 Lance is able to use trial and error to find a solution to the challenge he has, which is how to make the toy fire truck make a noise. The solution is pressing the red circle button on top of the fire truck.

As a parent, you play a key role in how your child develops problem-solving skills and how many times he will attempt to figure out a solution to a challenge. For example, your toddler has been attempting to open the closet door for a while. As he watches and studies you opening the closet door numerous times, he's finally able to open it himself. This is learning by imitating and observing problem solving in action.

Manipulating objects occurs when parents allow their toddlers to explore the object first. For example, Lance's mother could have pushed the button on the toy fire truck for him, but instead she allows time for her child to explore the toy and find the button so he can push it himself.

It is best to give your toddler the opportunity to solve the problem first before you intervene. If Lance continues to have a hard time, his mother can support him by turning the toy in a position that will allow him to notice and push the button himself. This will build your child's self-confidence and self-esteem as well as support the development of problem-solving skills.

Problem solving requires your child to use reasoning, decision-making, critical thinking, and creative thinking skills.

Your child will have so many problems to solve! As a parent, you can help by providing opportunities for open-ended exploration and by offering help. Give your child materials from around the house and let him make choices about how to use those materials. There are endless ways your child can explore plastic bowls, boxes, and scarves.

Sit back as you watch your child explore spatial relationships through problem solving by providing him with a spaghetti strainer and plastic straws as he tries to stick the straws through the holes of the strainer. Remember to keep your problem-solving activities simple. **More complex problem solving will happen when your child grows older.**

> It is important to always encourage and praise your child when he engages in problem-solving tasks and activities. This will leave your child feeling confident in his accomplishments and excited about solving more challenges.

Symbolic Play >
Pretend Play

Pretend play is when your child uses objects in make-believe activities.

Symbolic play is when she imitates actions and sounds she encounters in everyday life and imagines scenarios that take familiar experiences in a new direction.

"I am Mommy."

ACTIVITY

Rachel is in the closet of her mother's room. She finds some hats, shoes, purses, and a dress on the floor of the closet. Mom asks, "Rachel! What are you doing in the closet?" Mom does not hear a response.

Rachel begins to put her feet in her mom's shoes. She puts on her mom's dress by just putting her arms in any opening she can find, and then tops it all off with a hat. She comes out of the closet and stands in front of her parents. Rachel says, "I am Mommy," as she walks around the room.

INSIGHT

Rachel dresses up like her mother because these are clothes that she sees her mother wearing every day. Rachel is pretending to experiment with being Mommy. The clothing and accessories she puts on are all symbols she associates with Mom.

TODDLER > COGNITIVE DEVELOPMENT

Pretend play allows your child to experiment with different experiences that have occurred in her environment. A child may push a block around the floor as a car or put it to her ear as a cell phone.

Pretend play supports creativity, language skills, and the understanding of social roles. Whether you have a girl or a boy, it is important for you to have dress up clothes for your child, as they provide one of the easiest forms of pretend play.

Since your child's daily routines are now more structured, you have to be intentional in exposing your child to pretend play opportunities. That is because pretend play is a crucial part of your child's development in all areas and will continue to evolve. As your child approaches 18 months, she will use more imagination during her play experiences, using a broom to row her boat made from a box she is sitting in. During this time you will see your child engaged in solitary pretend play experiences.

From ages three to five this pretend play will expand to include others and children assigning roles to one another. Pretend play provides a fun way for you to interact with your child. Get in on the fun and see what happens.

Why support pretend play?

* It exposes your child to new vocabulary, such as *dog*, *cat*, or *princess* and *king*.
* You will help her learn to play with others during group play experiences. This helps develop her ability to take others' perspectives into account and learn empathy.

Objects to support pretend play:

* play dishes and play food
* toy toolbox
* pretend doctor's kit
* dress-up clothing

Some of the best toys to support your child during pretend play should be everyday materials found around your home. A large cardboard box can expand your child's thinking to turn it into a rocket ship or a racecar. Providing a laundry basket will encourage your child to think about how it can be used as a cage for his stuffed animals.

2. Social-Emotional Development

> **Social-emotional development refers to your child's ability to understand the feelings of others, manage strong emotions and expressions in a positive way, and start and keep relationships.**

This stage of development for a toddler is unique and special. It starts with a loving relationship between you and your child; you give him a sense of comfort, safety, confidence, and encouragement. It can also be a difficult stage because toddlers see things in their own way and have strong feelings, which makes it difficult to understand what toddlers need from you.

CHAPTER TWO > SOCIAL-EMOTIONAL DEVELOPMENT 23

WHOLE CHILD: TODDLER
Social-Emotional Development Components

1. Social Development

Social development involves playing and interacting with peers and having the desire to interact with other adults through story time, sharing, playing, and imitation. Imitation and pretending are used during social development to help toddlers understand social norms.

2. Emotional Development

Emotional development occurs when your child learns to use words to express feelings or thoughts. He is also learning about other people's feelings and how his behavior affects you.

3. Self-Regulation

Self-regulation includes a range of traits and abilities involving your child, especially being able to focus his attention, control emotions, and manage behavior and feelings.

4. Self-Awareness

Self-awareness is when your child realizes that he is a unique individual whose body, mind, and actions are separate from other people's. This is a very big milestone because it leads to the development of self-esteem.

TODDLER > SOCIAL-EMOTIONAL DEVELOPMENT 25

Social-emotional development starts with parents, family, and caregivers lovingly interacting with a child.

Social Development >
Relationships with Others

Social development involves your child having the skills he needs to form positive relationships with peers and family members.

ACTIVITY

Nolan and his dad go to a family barbeque at the park on Sunday. During the drive in the car, Nolan is having a good time and singing along to the music.

When the two of them arrive at the park, Nolan becomes very quiet and stops singing.

"Nolan, we're here!" Dad says. Nolan puts his head down. "Nolan, look! Your cousin is here! Don't be sad, I'm here with you." Nolan jumps out of the car seat, climbs down and clings to his cousin, hugging her as tightly as he can.

"Nolan, play," says his cousin. Nolan still hugs his cousin tightly for a few more minutes until Dad comes over with a toy truck. "You can go play," says Dad. Nolan looks up at Dad again then lets go of his cousin and takes the truck with his cousin to the sand box.

INSIGHT

Nolan is given support when Dad tells him that his cousin is here and he is going to play with her. Because he feels supported and trusts that his dad is in close proximity, Nolan feels comfortable cementing a relationship with his cousin.

Social relationships help your child gain trust, confidence, and security—all of which are important for him to explore his environment, learn, interact, and build relationships with others.

Your child needs to learn to trust very early in life. When your child feels that he can trust you and other familiar people, then he will be more willing and open to meeting new people and peers. This is because your child understands that you will always be nearby to provide support when needed.

Relationships with your child first consist of meeting your child's basic needs through sensitive caregiving. **By responding in a warm, loving, and gentle way, you're helping your child learn about communication, behavior, and emotions,** making him feel safe and secure, and promoting a strong relationship between you and him.

Those relationships let children express themselves—a cry, a laugh, a question—and get something back: a cuddle, a smile, an answer.

If these needs are consistently met, trust develops. Secure attachment relationships provide your child with feelings of self-worth and confidence. What children "get back" gives them very important information about what the world is like and how to act in the world.

At this age, your child is happier playing next to rather than with a peer. He will imitate what he sees another child doing without interacting with him. Play at this stage of development is called "parallel play" in which toddlers will play next to each other but not with each other.

During this stage of development it is essential to make sure your child is encouraged (praised), loved (hugs and kisses), and can develop trust and security with you (needs being consistently met).

Playing with peers will help teach him key social skills such as how to be kind, to share, and to resolve conflict; however, it's too early to expect them to play together; this will not happen until around two and a half years of age.

Regarding Nolan's trip to the family barbeque, note that when he became quiet he was experiencing a bit of separation anxiety. Separation anxiety occurs when there is a physical separation between him or her and you. This is a normal experience for your child to have when he has formed positive social relationships with his parents and others he sees on a regular basis.

A securely attached child will miss his parents when separated and will welcome the parents' or caregiver's reappearance or staying in close proximity. **As your child grows older separation anxiety will lessen;** instead, he will use other skills such as language, eye contact, and gestures to stay connected to you. Yet even with these newest social skills, your child will continue to seek physical closeness to you.

Emotional Development >
Calming Emotions

Emotional development refers to your child's ability to control his feelings and the ways he reacts to the feelings he has.

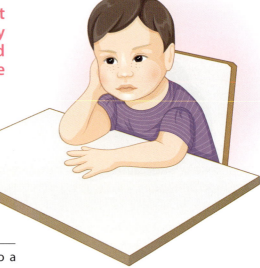

ACTIVITY

Sean's mom takes him to a playgroup at the local community center. Sean immediately heads toward the table with play dough. He sits down to play alongside his friend Zach.

Zach reaches out and grabs all of Sean's play dough. Sean quietly looks off into the distance, rests his head on his hand, and sits. The teacher asks Sean if everything is okay.

Sean, with a few tears rolling down his cheeks, points to the play dough in front of Zach. The teacher says to Sean, "I can see you are feeling sad. It is okay to feel sad when someone takes something from you."

INSIGHT

Zach knows it is not okay to take the play dough from his friend, but does not have the impulse control to stop his behavior. Sean is sad, but reacts quietly, while the teacher helps Sean identify that he is feeling sad, and validates his feelings.

It is important that you help your child name his feelings (happy, sad, frustrated) and express himself in a positive way. Your child's ability to express how he is feeling in a positive or appropriate way will have an impact on how relationships are formed with peers, family, and other people in his environment.

Toddlers haven't yet learned how to control their emotions, and mood swings can be alarmingly rapid and intense. But they are also—thankfully—short-lived, moving from screaming in frustration to smiling and playing within seconds. Staying calm, helping them with the source of frustration, and using distraction techniques ("Oh, look, a red leaf!") will help them. Don't expect miracles though—plenty of five year olds still have difficulty controlling their emotions.

Self-Regulation >
Self-Control

Self-regulation involves your child's ability to gain control of her bodily functions (e.g. mastering potty training), managing emotions (e.g. controlling tantrums), keeping focused (e.g. waiting for something she wants), and paying attention.

"Dolly, Mommy, dolly!"

You can support your child's ability to achieve a level of calmness and bring herself into a calm state by giving soft touches on the back or by providing a favorite soft blanket for her to cuddle and hold.

ACTIVITY

Lilly is at the store with her mom, and she sees a doll that she wants on the shelf. "Dolly, Mommy, dolly," Lilly says.

"No, Lilly we are not buying any dollies today," Mom replies. Lilly begins to have a tantrum in the store, screaming for the doll she can't have.

INSIGHT

Because Lilly has just turned 13 months old, she is still learning how to regulate her emotions and understand that she cannot have everything she wants. This kind of reaction is normal for a toddler. Mom knows that she is not going to buy the doll, but she also does not want Lilly to scream and cry in the store.

Mom has to take a deep breath and keep herself calm, even though she is embarrassed by the situation. By doing this, she can then focus on getting Lilly to calm down as well.

Tips

Support your child in times of difficulty. If your child has a hard time when you say "no" to something, remain compassionate and empathetic. When it comes to tantrums, the most common parenting advice given is to ignore the tantrums and they will go away. This is not the best advice because it can make your child feel undervalued or unsupported. **It is important to acknowledge your child's feelings** by saying, "I understand you are sad" and waiting nearby for the difficult behavior to subside. Toddlers have a hard time because they are still trying to figure out who they are and develop their sense of identity in the world.

Offer emotional support to help your child work through his challenges. Arrange plenty of downtime between activities.

Offer a five-minute warning, then a two-minute warning, then a ten-second warning to help your child transition between one activity to another. These are simple actions that can help your child cope and calm down.

When your toddler has a tantrum, the following coping mechanisms will help you:

* See the tantrum from your child's point of view. Tantrums can occur because your child is tired or hungry, causing her not to feel well or to be irritated. As you see the situation from your toddler's point of view, you will have compassion to be able to deal with her tantrums.

* Remember, you always have options. If a tantrum begins somewhere in public, you don't have to stay. Feel comfortable picking up your child and going home. Sometimes a good nap will help, and you can try again another day.

* Consider whether saying "no" is absolutely necessary. What alternatives are there? You may be saying "no" to candy at the store, but perhaps you could say "yes" to fruit, some crackers, or another healthful treat.

ACTIVITY

Caleb comes out of his bedroom and goes to the kitchen to see his mom. "Hungry, Mommy!" says Caleb.

Mom replies, "I am making dinner now, Caleb." She rubs his back. "It will be a few minutes." Caleb goes back to his room.

A few minutes pass and Mom says, "Caleb! It's time for dinner. Come eat!"

Caleb runs into the kitchen. He stops right in front of Mom who is standing two feet away from his highchair. She hands Caleb his plate of food, he walks slowly while holding the plate with two hands to his highchair. He then puts the plate of food on the tray of his chair and climbs in. Mom pushes the tray so it locks on the highchair and says, "I hope you like it!"

INSIGHT

Through a structured routine (having set times for activities and events, like meals) Mom is supporting Caleb's self-regulation skills. Caleb is learning how to control his natural reaction of distress when he is hungry by being gently encouraged to wait a few short minutes for his mom to finish preparing his food.

Caleb's mom is also encouraging Caleb's independence by letting him put his plate of food on his highchair tray.

Encouraging your child's independence is not an easy job; it takes patience. But the long-term benefits are worth it. Your patience with and support of your child will help him gain mastery over self-regulation skills and become more independent.

The good news is that your child is at the age when he wants to have more independence and learn how to do things himself (putting on socks or carrying his plate to his chair). At first the desire and need for greater independence can lead to a struggle between your desires and the desires of your child. This can lead to screams, tears, and frustration. This age period is commonly described as the "terrible twos" (even though these types of independence-seeking behaviors start when your child is a toddler). Tantrums can be extremely difficult to manage. Your child will stomp his feet, kick his legs, yell, and throw things.

Realistic expectations, patience, and sensitive guidance on your part are important for your child and can help make the "terrible twos" pretty terrific!

TODDLER > SOCIAL-EMOTIONAL DEVELOPMENT 33

Allowing your toddler to exercise independence will give him confidence and build self-esteem.

Remember, the Whole Child Parenting Program offers appropriate developmental products and monthly activity books that walk you through supporting your child's skills. Using these in conjunction with the recommended age-appropriate room materials ensures faster development.

Self-Awareness >
Self-Perception

Self-awareness involves your child learning about herself, such as how her body moves, what she likes and dislikes, as well as what she can and cannot do.

Self-awareness is the physical realization that your child is separated from you. She may have similar features as you (hands, hair, feet) but her features look different from yours. A lot of these physical realizations occur when your child looks at herself in the mirror and in pictures, and when she learns to identify her own name.

During this age, your child will demonstrate self-awareness skills by using words such as *I* and *mine*. You will hear your child describe her own interests ("I paint") and skills ("I jump"). This differentiation is one of the developments that will lead your child to developing self-esteem.

It then becomes your responsibility as a parent to support your child with verbal feedback and praise. You can say things like, "Yes, you can jump!" and "Yes, you can paint."

Building self-esteem supports your child's emotional health because it makes your child feel good about herself and understand she can do something on her own. This is critical in developing relationships with others and having the "I can do it" spirit.

TODDLER > SOCIAL-EMOTIONAL DEVELOPMENT

As your child matures and reaches two, she will begin to see that even though she has features similar to those around her, she is an individual with her own personality and identity. With your support, your child will feel good about who she is as she becomes more aware of herself and the world around her. **Celebrate your child's personality as she grows day by day.**

> **There are several activities that will encourage self-awareness in your child:**
>
> * Have photos of your child next to pictures that he draws and display his artwork on your refrigerator door or wall.
>
> * Hold a mirror in front of him and have him point to his eyes, nose, mouth, and ears. Talk about the color of his hair and the color of your hair. You can even sing the song and play "Head and Shoulders, Knees and Toes."

ACTIVITY

Ethan is in the living room while his dad is watching TV. Ethan sees a man dancing on TV and decides he wants to try to do some of the same moves. Ethan starts to wiggle his fingers and clap his hands. As Ethan watches the man on TV, he sees the man move a finger in a way Ethan has never tried before to a song Ethan has never heard before.

Ethan looks at his hand and starts moving his finger up and down like the man on TV.

INSIGHT

By watching the man on TV, Ethan learns about the parts of his own body and how they move.

3. Language Development

> **Language development occurs when toddlers add new words to their growing vocabulary. From age one to three, children will learn 1,000 to 2,000 new words.**

Your child can learn language easily; this is also a critical time to acquire language before this ability gets less acute with age.

As your child approaches age three, his language skills will become more fluent. Therefore, it is very important for parents to engage in continuous language exchanges with their toddlers. For example, talk while doing things and going places, and expand on basic words your toddler says. If he says "car," you should respond, "Yes, that is a red car." These types of activities and reinforcement build your toddler's language skills.

CHAPTER THREE > LANGUAGE DEVELOPMENT

Whole Child: toddler
Language Development Components

You will often hear your child say "wawa" for water. Focus on the effort your child is making at being understood, not how he is saying the word. You can then engage in a language experience by saying, "Yes, this is water." No matter what stage of language development your toddler is in, remember to help build his language skills by using simple language yourself. But don't use "baby" language when communicating with your child. You want to help him learn language correctly.

1. Listening and Understanding

Listening leads to your child becoming a good reader, good speaker, and understanding what you and other adults are saying. Teaching listening skills will help your child develop language and social skills.

2. Communication and Speaking

Communication involves the use of single words in combination with gestures. Toddlers speak using two- to three-word sentences to communicate with a specific purpose.

3. Emerging Literacy

Emerging literacy at this age develops from learning book-handling skills, having books read aloud, listening and talking, observing parents reading and writing, storytelling, and experiencing rich literacy environments.

Interacting with the world around her by identifying and naming objects and images will help her build her language skills faster.

Listening and Understanding >
Hearing

"My toes!"

Listening and understanding is when attention is given to the things that we hear and how we subsequently make meaning and comprehend what we have heard.

ACTIVITY

Bella is on the floor playing a game with Mom. Mom asks, "Bella, where are your toes?" Bella lifts up her foot and with her hand on her toes she says, "Here Bella's toes."

Mom then asks Bella, "Can you find the toes on your other foot?" Bella starts to lift up the same foot to show her mom her toes again. Bella says, "My toes!"

Mom then points to Bella's other foot to show Bella what she is asking and asks the question again.

INSIGHT

Bella is listening to her mom each time, but she does not respond correctly both times. The first time she is asked to find her toes, Bella understands the question. The second time Bella does not understand that the question has changed, and that she is being asked to find the toes on her other foot. When a parent can rephrase a question or use gestures to show alternate meaning, she is giving her child the chance to understand and act on her own.

The more opportunities your child has to listen to lots of people talking—verbal communication between people in her environment—the better chance she has of understanding what she hears.

Because Bella is still developing her listening and understanding skills, Mom needs to provide more support to her by using a gesture to help clarify her question and asking the question again.

Sometimes it seems like your child is not listening to you. That is because listening requires attention and focus, and these are skills your child is still developing. This is why making eye contact with your child when speaking becomes so important. It will help him listen better and understand what you are saying when you are able to grab his attention.

There are several techniques you can use when supporting your child's listening and understanding skills.

Like Bella's mom in the example, give your child a visual cue by pointing to the object or area you are talking about. Also, when giving one-step directions ("Bring your shoes, please.") reinforce what you asked ("What did Mommy ask you to bring?"). This will let you know if your child understands what you are saying or if you need to give a visual cue by pointing to the object.

With your support as your child matures, his ability to listen and understand will increase. **Remember, listening and understanding lead to greater cognitive development.**

Communication and Speaking >
Speaking

Communication and speaking reflect your child's abilities to give a message to another person through nonverbal cues (or sign language) and spoken words.

Communication and speaking also build self esteem in your child as she learns that her voice can be heard.

The ability of your child to communicate is important in relationships they will form with adults and peers. Communication in all its forms plays a key role in increasing her ability to use language effectively.

Keep in mind that you won't understand all of your toddler's words, at least at first. She still has trouble producing many sounds, so she may substitute the sound of "b" for "d," and so on.

Your toddler might say, "Dat otay," and that is appropriate at this age. What's important, and worth celebrating, is her effort at being understood.

Just as your child needs nourishing food to build physical strength, she also needs linguistic nutrition (words for her vocabulary bank) for strong development of language, communication, and cognitive skills. The more you speak with your child the more she will learn to communicate with you.

Talk during daily routines about how you prepare the apple for snack by cutting it in half and how you clean up by wiping off the counter with a kitchen towel when you are done. Speak clearly, making face-to-face contact with your child.

Remember that every toddler is different; some develop their language skills at a steady pace and others do so in spurts.

ACTIVITY

 Ava is sitting on the floor of her living room with Dad. Dad says, "Ava, it is time for your nap. Nap time for Ava."

Ava replies, "No rib!" for crib. "Ava, no ap!" for nap.

INSIGHT

 With these simple words Ava demonstrates to her dad that she is building her word bank (*crib*, *nap*, *no*) to communicate that she does not want to take a nap right now.

Sign Language

Sign language uses facial, hand, and body movements as a way to communicate with others and helps your child develop her social and emotional skills by giving her another way to communicate, especially when she becomes frustrated.

The biggest benefit to teaching your child sign language, especially if she is a visual learner (because it uses both hearing and seeing), is that it boosts your child's cognitive development as she develops language and reasoning skills.

As you teach your child sign language, it is important not to focus on whether your child is producing the precise sign (exactly how it should look). The focus must be on celebrating that your child is communicating her needs to you when she otherwise would have used only verbal language, which is often not developed enough for her to communicate exactly what she wants.

ACTIVITY

Mom notices Sophia is not using many words when interacting with others. For this reason Mom decides to learn about baby sign language so that she can start teaching Sophia.

Mom starts learning and teaching simple signs to Sophia, ones she can use to say things that she wants or needs. Mom is looking forward to the time when she can see Sophia use the signs independently.

Mom and Sophia arrive home from a birthday party at her cousin's house on the other side of town. Mom gets Sophia out of the car seat, and they walk through the door. Once home, Sophia sits on the floor and does the sign for *sleep*. Then she follows by saying, "Seepy."

Mom is so excited that Sophia has used both the sign and the spoken word that she scoops up Sophia to give her a great big hug.

INSIGHT

Through a modified from of the sign for *sleep* and the use of the spoken word, Sophia communicates to Mom so that she can get her needs met.

Sleepy.

Emergent Literacy >
I Can "Read"!

Emergent or emerging literacy involves how your child interacts with books and when reading and writing, even though your child cannot yet read and write in the standard sense.

Emerging literacy refers to your child's knowledge of reading and writing skills before he actually learns how to read and write words. Emergent literacy involves the process of being literate.

Nursery rhymes are short and have a repetition of sounds and words in attractive, easy-to-copy rhythms. **Rhymes are important because parents and children can say them at any time and in any place.** Rhymes need no toys or even a book; they depend on the sound of the voice. And you can practice them in the car, at the store, or on the playground.

By playing with rhymes, your child will discover how language works and become familiar with the relationship between sounds and letters, which helps when he begins to read.

The good news is that adults can have fun with rhymes and rhyming stories as well.

ACTIVITY

Take a moment and have your child sit with you on the couch. Get comfy. Read this little rhyme to your child while you wiggle each one of his fingers or toes.

"This Little Piggy"

This little piggy went to market.
This little piggy stayed home.
This piggy had roast beef.
This little piggy had none.
And this little piggy cried,
   "Wee! Wee! Wee!" all
   the way home.

INSIGHT

The rhyme "This Little Piggy" allows your child to play with repetition and language sounds such as "wee." Sharing "This Little Piggy" and other nursery rhymes and nursery songs supports emergent literacy.

TODDLER > LANGUAGE DEVELOPMENT 45

When introducing rhymes, use popular rhyming books, then let your child explore the pages. Use exaggerated speech to make the words come alive. Add music if you have it, and you can sing rhyming songs together.

Remember, the Whole Child Parenting Program offers appropriate developmental products and monthly activity books that walk you through supporting your child's skills. Using these in conjunction with the recommended age-appropriate room materials ensures faster development.

4. Creative Development

> **Creative play and creative activities are important to your child's overall development. They help grow imagination and also develop problem-solving, thinking, and motor skills.**

Drama, music, dance, and visual arts promote the development of creativity and imagination in toddlers. These activities also help toddlers develop their senses through exploration and discovery.

Your child can use creative play to communicate his feelings. He might not always be able to explain verbally why he's feeling angry, sad, happy, or frightened, but in an encouraging environment, he might be able to express these feelings using paint, color, movement, or music. Toddlers often use both hands equally when they're painting or drawing, so you cannot yet tell whether your toddler is right handed or left handed. This usually becomes more obvious at about three or four years of age, though a preference can emerge as early as 13 months. The most important issue is that you provide as many opportunities as possible for your child to develop his creativity.

CHAPTER FOUR > CREATIVE DEVELOPMENT　　　　47

 Dramatic Play
 Music
 Visual Arts
 Dance

Whole Child: toddler
Creative Development Components

1. Music

Toddlers are continuously moving, so incorporate free dance while exposing your child to different styles of music. Start to observe your child's favorite song or genre of music. Play with different percussion instruments and start to teach your child about *loud* and *soft*.

2. Dance

Dance with your child in your arms or separately. Take time to imitate your child's movements so he knows you are present. At this age, your child can recognize his hands and feet. Play games by waving your hands or stomping your feet.

3. Visual Arts

Art is messy. Expect to see your child scribble, smash paint, and explore materials like paper and paint brushes. Art supports self-confidence as your child is allowed to create anything his mind can think of. These projects also engage fine motor skills so that your child will develop the skills needed for writing.

4. Dramatic Play

This is the age when your child starts to show preferences. Have props such as puppets, hats, and clothes from Mom or Dad. Encouragement in creativity is key at this stage as your child is taking cues from the adults around him.

TODDLER > CREATIVE DEVELOPMENT   49

Your home can provide innumerable opportunities for children to experiment and play, encouraging them to express their creativity and imagination.

Remember, the Whole Child Parenting Program offers appropriate developmental products and monthly activity books that walk you through supporting your child's skills. Using these in conjunction with the recommended age-appropriate room materials ensures faster development.

Music >
Vocal or Instrumental Sounds

Music is sound made by instruments or vocals or a combination of both.

As your child listens to or creates music, you will see her express her physical abilities and emotions by how she moves her body. Music is appealing to your child as well because it is something she can do independently. By showing her independence and expressing her creativity, your child is able to learn more about herself.

Developing a personal preference for different types of music starts when you are young. When children listen to certain styles of music repeatedly, they learn to like or prefer one style to another. This preference carries through to adulthood. Based upon this, it is very important to expose your toddler to many different types of music so that her repertoire will not be limited to only one genre.

Music will enable your child to develop physically as well. This can be observed when you see your child shaking her hips from side to side or when dancing with her legs slightly bent and apart. Your child is developing her large muscles in the hip area, strengthening her leg muscles, and continuing to develop her balancing skills.

You can encourage your child to move to the rhythm of the music by counting with her as she shakes side to side ("One and shake, two and shake, shake, shake, shake."). By doing this, you encourage math skills as well.

TODDLER > CREATIVE DEVELOPMENT

ACTIVITY

Mom takes Harper to a mommy and me music class. They are running a little late, so when they arrive, Harper is anxious to go in.

Class has already started and the song playing is "The Ants Go Marching." Harper and Mom are each given a yellow and green scarf to wave around during the song.

Everyone in the class is encouraged to wave their scarves and march around the room to the sound of the beat expressed in the song as "Boom! Boom! Boom!"

All of a sudden the song starts to get slower and slower. Harper sees her mom start to march slower and slower, so she follows along; however, the pace is too slow for Harper, so she begins to march fast again, saying "Boom! Boom! Boom!"

INSIGHT

Through this activity Harper gets to interact with music that makes her move fast then slowly. She also gets to develop her physical skills by waving the scarf around and moving her legs up and down. The song brings out emotions of happiness as Harper gets excited and wants to keep marching fast.

Music really does open the mind and stimulate the body.

Dance >
Moving Lively

Dance is an excellent way for toddlers to develop gross motor skills as they move and thinking skills as they consider the move they will make next.

Activities like dancing will cause your child to think about balancing, moving, and shaking all at the same time. Often you will notice your child having difficulty and wanting to focus on one thing (like shaking the hips). This is okay because he is still building up his dance skills.

When your child hears music, it makes him want to dance without any prompting from you. Dance moves may only consist of him bobbing up and down with his feet planted on the ground. Your child is just enjoying the fact that he can bob up and down, shake, and move his feet without falling down. **As your child matures, you will see him combine moving side to side with circling around. As he moves into age two, you will notice that the arms are incorporated in his moves.** He's having fun, too!

Your child loves having a dance

TODDLER > CREATIVE DEVELOPMENT

partner. Set a time during the day to dance with your child to different genres of music. You may be surprised by how much rhythm you have!

As you encourage dancing in your child, you also encourage him to express himself and be creative. This will help him later in life as he learns to improve his coordination, build his spatial awareness skills, and think through ways of how to move his body.

ACTIVITY

It is a rainy day and Jaxon cannot go outside. Mom thinks it is a great time to turn up the music and let her little dancer twist and shout.

Jaxon loves to listen to very fast music, so Mom picks a playlist or CD with fast music. As soon as the music starts, Jaxon quickly throws out his arms, stands with his legs apart, and starts twisting his body and shaking his hips, legs, and arms as fast as he can.

From time to time Mom will join Jaxon and move with him to the song. On this occasion, Mom just wants to sit back and watch him let loose.

INSIGHT

When Jaxon was an infant he responded to dance and music by smiling and perhaps even clapping his hands. Now that he is walking on his own two feet, he has enough control over his body to do some more complex toddler dancing that involves more body parts.

Visual Arts >
Art I Can See

Visual arts for young children include anything they can see and create.

Visual arts can include scribbles on a piece of paper, a painting, her hand- or footprint, as well as coloring a picture, just to name a few options. **Visual arts reflect the world your child is in.**

Engaging in visual art supports your child's experience with different textures (e.g. crinkled paper or glue on paper) as well as developing fine motor skills, because so many art creations are done using hands (painting and coloring). **Your child is able to express herself by making choices such as what colors of paint to use or by combining different mediums.** When you give your child visual art experiences, you will help her gain a better understanding of her creative abilities.

Give your child experiences that are focused on the exploration of materials and textures.

Experiences should include some of the following examples:

* Finger painting, which supports not only the development of visual arts but also understanding cause and effect.

* Shaving cream painting on a cookie sheet to support the development of the senses when she experiments with the texture of the shaving cream.

* Taping a large piece of paper to the table and leaving it there for a couple days. This gives your child the opportunity to engage in visual arts any time by being able to come and go as she pleases.

ACTIVITY

Traci and Mom have just come home from a new art exhibit at the children's museum. Mom wants to give Traci an opportunity to create her own art, so she goes into her office and comes out with a very large piece of white paper. Mom places the paper on the highchair in front of Traci and tapes down each of the four corners so the paper will be secure. Next Mom gives Traci a bit of yellow paint in a cup and puts the cup on the tray of the highchair next to the paper.

Traci begins to dip her hands in the cup and then slaps her hands down on the paper. Then after Traci puts her hands in the yellow paint again, she starts to touch her clothes and her face. By the time Traci is done, everything is yellow.

INSIGHT

Mom does not mind that Traci gets so messy. She is more excited that Traci is able to explore the paint and experiment with all the different places she can put it.

Visual art includes not only things that your child creates, but also art your child can see in a museum or outside at the park. Take a trip with your child to your local art museum. Seeing the works of other artists will open up your child's creative thinking. Support those skills by talking about the different art you see together at the museum (e.g. "Do you see the bird in the picture? It looks so shiny and like it is flying.")

Remember, no matter what your child does on paper, you do not need to insist on calling the image something or identifying it in any way. At this stage, she is only exploring, and the picture is not meant to represent something. When your child is finished creating a picture, talk about the colors she used (e.g. "I see you used yellow paint. It is very bright like the sun."). You can also talk about the different marks that were made on the paper (e.g. "I love your circles. Did you see you made a circle shape?").

At this age your child may not verbally say much about her creation, but by talking to her about her art, you are supporting her self-confidence and encouraging her to believe that she has the ability to create anything and do it well.

Dramatic Play >
Pretending

Your child will go to a place that allows him to pretend to be someone or something else.

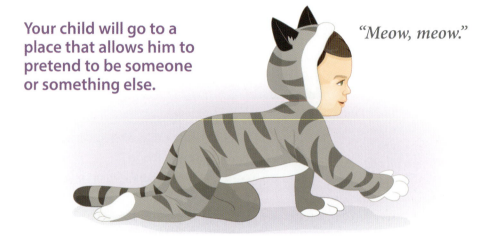

"Meow, meow."

ACTIVITY

Justin is looking out the window of his family room when he sees a black cat walking by. As the cat stops and comes up to the window, Justin begins to say, "Meow, meow." Then Justin begins to bang on the window, which makes the cat run away.

Justin runs out of the family room to his bedroom and opens his toy chest. He pulls out a cat costume he has from Halloween. Justin brings the cat suit to his mom so that she can help him put it on. Once Justin has the suit on, he gets on his hands and knees and begins to crawl back to the family room window saying, "Meow, meow."

INSIGHT

Justin loves to pretend to be something that he sees in his environment. Mom supports Justin's imagination by letting him put on the cat suit and reenact being a cat. Mom can make this dramatic play opportunity even more fun if she also pretends to be a cat with Justin.

TODDLER > CREATIVE DEVELOPMENT

Dramatic play is when your child recreates the world of home through pretend play scenarios (e.g. pretends to sip warm tea from a cup at the dinner table).

Dramatic play supports the development of language and words as well as thinking skills when your child considers what he wants to be. **Dramatic play also builds social skills as your child interacts with others.**

Your child loves to engage in dramatic play experiences because it includes social interactions with you and his peers. Social interaction really starts at birth; however, during this time, your infant wanted to engage in role play only with you. Now he may want to include interactions with peers. Dramatic play is unique in that it includes imitation and can take place individually or in a social setting.

Make sure you provide a space and opportunities for dramatic play in your home. One example of how you can do this is by building a cave or tunnel for your child using boxes or sheets. You can take a sheet and simply lay it over the couch and loveseat or over four chairs. Your child will love to crawl under the sheet while pretending to be a bear in the woods saying, "Grrrr!"

Dramatic play does not have to occur in only one part of your home; it can take place anywhere (outside, kitchen area, bathtub, or the living room). The only requirement is that it should be spontaneous, safe, and fun. **For extra fun, participate in pretend play with your child—a sure opportunity for laughter and bonding.**

> For your child, dramatic play will be brief; however, as your toddler matures, you will see him engage in longer dramatic play experiences with more details and accompanying language or even storytelling.

> Toddlers love dramatic play. If you see your child mimicking a cat, pretend to be a cat, too. Scurry around the house trying to chase a mouse.

5. Physical Development

> **Physical development includes your child's large muscle and small muscle skills.**

Walking is the main skill that most parents think about in this area as they look forward to the day their child starts to walk.

Your child will begin to demonstrate more advanced skills as he matures—such as pushing his feet on a ride-on toy, tossing a ball (you will be amazed by how far he can toss a ball), and jumping up and down in one place and landing on both feet. His ability to roll back and forth and go from a prone position to a standing position with no support makes this an exciting time.

You will also see your little one stacking blocks, pillows, and even books when he wants to climb on something.

He can use a spoon to feed himself and hold a drinking cup. Until you see all of these things, you do not realize just how much your toddler has grown from infancy to now.

Because of all of the advances your child has made, you will see that he has a greater desire for independence and will become more and more determined to do things his own way (e.g. attempt to climb up onto a picnic table).

CHAPTER FIVE > PHYSICAL DEVELOPMENT 59

WHOLE CHILD: TODDLER
Physical Development Components

1. Gross Motor Skills

A gross motor skill involves your child's ability to control arm and leg movements. This includes climbing, walking up and down stairs, kicking a ball, carrying large items, running short distances, and standing on tiptoes.

2. Fine Motor Skills

Fine motor development applies to small movements of the hands, wrists, fingers, feet, and toes. Fine motor development also includes the smaller actions of grasping an object between the thumb and a finger or using the lips and the tongue to taste an object.

3. Sensory Motor Skills

Sensory motor skills include the five areas of taste, touch, hearing, smelling, and seeing and how they interact with objects and actions in the child's environment. Touch involves games that use the muscles; sight can be used to complete a maze or dot-to-dot puzzle; hearing might include playing listening games; smell can be used to go on a smell walk; and taste can involve trying frozen versus hot foods.

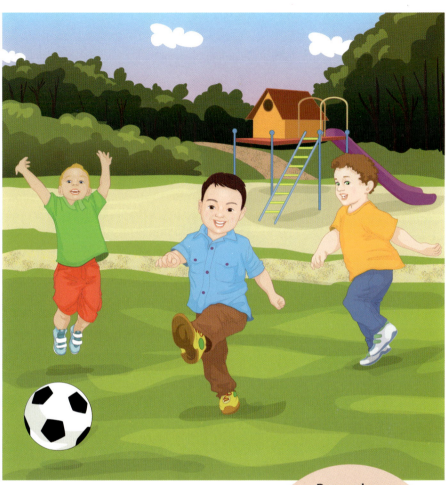

Parents and children spending time playing physical games and doing activities together is one of the best ways to help children develop gross and fine motor skills.

Remember, the Whole Child Parenting Program offers appropriate developmental products and monthly activity books that walk you through supporting your child's skills. Using these in conjunction with the recommended age-appropriate room materials ensures faster development.

Gross Motor Skills >
Large Muscles

Gross motor skills are movements that help your child develop large muscle control in the arms and legs.

Your child will use his body to learn how to interact with large objects in his environment (e.g. stairs on a jungle gym).

Gross motor development plays a role in making sure that your child remains healthy as he keeps his body moving. Physical abilities that are examples of gross motor development include crawling, walking, jumping, and rolling. An example of a jumping activity you can do with your child at home is hopping up and down like a frog.

ACTIVITY

Mom and Brandon are on the floor of the living room doing some stretches and exercises together. Mom lies down on the floor like a log and rolls toward the couch.

"Your turn," Mom says to Brandon. Mom helps Brandon lie down on the floor to stretch his arms up and keep his legs straight like a log. Then Mom gives Brandon a little push so that he rolls along the floor.

As Brandon begins to roll over, he immediately puts his feet up and arm out, causing him to stop. Brandon then continues to rock back and forth from one side to the other with his feet in the air.

INSIGHT

With this simple movement, Brandon is demonstrating his gross motor skills. His waist and legs are moving together; however, at this age, Brandon is unaware that keeping his legs in the air stops his ability to roll over completely. Brandon wants to put his arms and legs out because he thinks that he will keep rolling and not stop. When Brandon gets older and has more control over his gross motor movements he will feel more comfortable letting himself roll.

Your toddler is still exploring his gross motor movements and experimenting with using different parts of his body in new ways. Because your child is still developing his balance and coordination it is important that you provide support by letting your child know that you are present to help him safely test his physical limits. This will build trust between you and your toddler and make him feel more confident in further practicing and developing his gross motor movements.

Fine Motor Skills >
Small Muscles

Fine motor development occurs when your child uses her small muscles (fingers and hands) to engage in activities.

ACTIVITY

Dana is sitting with her parents at the dinner table. Mom gives Dana a spoon to eat her yogurt. At first Dana ignores the spoon and puts her hand in the bowl of yogurt, scooping the yogurt and bringing her hand to her mouth to lick her fingers.

"Dana, here is your spoon," Mom says as she gets up from the table and stands behind Dana. Mom then puts the spoon in Dana's hand, and with her hand on top of Dana's hand helps Dana bring the spoon to the bowl to scoop the yogurt. Then while still having her hand on Dana's hand, Mom brings the spoon to Dana's mouth so she can eat the yogurt. After Dana eats the spoonful of yogurt, Mom says, "You did it, Dana! Good job!"

Mom sits back down at the table and watches to see if Dana will use the spoon on her own. Dana takes the spoon and holds it with her fist. With her fist toward the base of the spoon, Dana dips the spoon in the yogurt and brings it to her mouth. Mom claps and says, "Good job!"

INSIGHT

Mom supports Dana by showing her how to use the spoon. Mom reinforces her encouragement of Dana by giving her praise, which entices Dana to want to continue to explore and try to use the spoon herself.

Fine motor development includes smiling, grasping, opening and closing hands, waving, and picking up an eating utensil or pencil.

As your child grows so do her fine motor skills. You will see your child learning to do more with her hands. There are several things that your child should accomplish by the age of two in this area; one of those is being able to eat using utensils.

At this time your child is exploring her ability to feed herself with the use of a spoon. She will have some spilling, may miss her mouth from time to time, and may even use her hand to scoop food into her spoon. These are all age-appropriate examples of how your child is still developing grasping and scooping, and testing wrist movements and finger strength.

Many times parents do not give their toddlers a utensil because they feel like their child will be messy; however for a child to master eating with utensils, you must provide opportunities for self-feeding during daily meal times. The more practice you give the better your child will get.

There are many other ways parents can support fine motor skills. One way is by reading books together. Let your child use her pointer finger to point to pictures in the book and turn the pages. If she is not pointing to pictures, you can model first and then have her imitate you.

Give your child opportunities to work on fine motor skills during routines like taking off her socks. Your toddler will be able to grasp her socks and pull them off; this skill requires hand-eye coordination. You will observe your child grasp the sock with her whole hand; this is normal as her pincer grasp is still developing. **The pincer grasp involves using the thumb and pointer finger or the thumb and middle fingers to pick up and hold.**

When your child reaches age two she has developed more finger strength and will start to grasp writing utensils and eating utensils in a pincer grasp. When your child develops more finger strength, she no longer needs to use her whole fist to control the movement of a writing utensil, such as a crayon, and can begin making more detailed and precise marks when drawing. **It is important to remember that fine motor skills do not develop overnight,** and it is crucial that you support your child by providing fine motor skill development opportunities as part of your daily routines.

Sensory Motor Skills >
Seeing and Moving

Sensory motor skills involve your child combining his senses with large and small muscle movements.

We know there are five senses:

1. taste (gustatory),
2. touch (tactile),
3. hearing (auditory),
4. sight (visual),
5. smell (olfactory).

Some example of how these five senses play a role in the development of gross motor and fine motor skills are:

* Touch: touches a ball and throws it;
* Hearing: listens to your request to jump up and down or sit down;
* Sight: sees where to kick the ball or how to grasp the paintbrush.

The first two years of your child's life are known as the sensorimotor stage. Your child needs to move his body and actively interact with his environment. Try to limit TV, electronic time, and other passive media sources. Interact with your child physically by playing games like kicking and throwing a ball together.

In addition to those five senses there are two more senses that are associated specifically with movement. They are **spatial sense** and **balance sense**.

Spatial sense lets your child know where his body is in relation to things

TODDLER > PHYSICAL DEVELOPMENT

around him. This sense can be observed when you see your toddler turn around and sit in a chair without falling down. It also contributes to your toddler's coordination skills. Without spatial sense, your toddler would be clumsy during movements and would move like a robot.

Balance sense is the movement of one part of the body while the rest stays in one place (lifting up one leg). Your child will stumble and fall sometimes; however, you should not see a pattern of this.

Pushing, pulling, twisting, turning, sitting, and rising are examples of the type of movements that develop balance and coordination skills in your toddler.

Encourage your child to use all of his senses to develop his motor skills by joining in the experience with him. Play games that require your child to listen and have physical contact with objects. Remember: What your child learns today will support his developmental successes in the future.

Based on your child's age, we know he will try the following as he discovers his gross motor abilities:

* try to balance himself with one foot up and hands in the air;
* attempt to climb objects (e.g. furniture, steps, simple climbing structures);
* hold objects or toys while walking (e.g. pulling a car by a string while walking around the room);
* ride a toy by using his hands or feet.

6. Health and Care

> **Your toddler is developing more teeth, growing longer hair, and adjusting to a new diet.**

Your child is on the move! She is pulling herself up, walking, reaching, and eating with her hands. Her daily schedules are changing along with her body. Your child is becoming more vocal and independent, which can come with some defiant and challenging behavior. There are a number of things you can do to help keep her clean and healthy from head to toe while avoiding big fights, struggles, and confrontations.

CHAPTER SIX > HEALTH AND CARE 69

WHOLE CHILD: TODDLER
Health and Care

Hygiene >
Hair, Skin, Eyes, Nails, Ears, and Tooth Care

Hair Care

Your two year old's oil glands on her scalp and body don't become fully functional until puberty, so shampoo only as needed. Once a week is usually plenty.

Brushing

Brushing hair can help bring oils to the surface of the scalp. When trying to get out knots and tangles, try using a detangling spray and a wide-toothed comb or a brush with round-tipped bristles. Start combing or brushing out the ends and then work your way up to the scalp to avoid tugging and pulling.

Working Together

* Let your child use the comb in her hair or on a doll before combing her hair yourself.

* When in the bath, let her run her fingers in the shampoo just like you would.

* Let her wash her doll's hair in the tub.

* Let your child watch you wash her hair by propping up a mirror in the bathtub.

* While rinsing, have your child tilt her head back and use a bucket to avoid getting shampoo in her sensitive eyes.

Skin Care

Dry skin and dehydration can occur due to the weather.

When cleaning dry skin:

* Pat down skin and make sure not to wipe rough, chapped skin (especially face and cheeks).
* Apply sunscreen when going outside because toddlers' sensitive skin can burn easily.

Caring for dry skin:

* Try cutting back on bath time and sticking to 10-minute baths.
* Using the moisturizer within minutes of taking your child out of the tub will seal in the water that's still in her skin from the bath.
* Choose a non-alcohol-based moisturizer, such as Aquaphor® Baby Healing Ointment or Cetaphil® Moisturizing Cream.
* Reapply moisturizers at least two or three times a day.
* Offer your child plenty of water year round to replace the moisture that's evaporating from her skin.
* Add more fatty foods to her diet, such as avocados, flax seed, and olive oil.

Eye Care

Provide sun protection when outdoors by getting in the habit of using UV coated kid's sunglasses. This is especially important if your child's eyes are lighter in color.

The presence of eye and vision problems is rare. Most little ones begin life with healthy eyes and start developing visual abilities with no problems.

You will see that your child's hand-eye coordination and depth perception are well developed by this time. Remember: Consult your pediatrician if you see any of the signs listed below.

Check your child's eyes regularly to see if:

* your child's eyes are crossed,
* they are sensitive to light,
* one eye is wandering,
* both eyes cannot follow an object as it moves back and forth in front of her.

Conjunctivitis (Pink Eye)

Conjunctivitis, commonly known as pink eye, is the swelling of the white part of the eye and the inner surface of the eyelid.

Conjunctivitis can cause parents to worry because the eye looks extremely red. It does spread very quickly and is fairly common. It does not cause long-term damage to the eye or your toddler's vision. Some types of pink eye will go away without treatment, but other types will need medical attention.

Symptoms usually include:
* watery discharge,
* veiny redness in the white area of an eye,
* itchy and swollen eyes,
* stringy discharge that causes eyelids to stick together, especially after sleeping.

Conjunctivitis has three forms: allergic, viral, or bacterial.

Allergic conjunctivitis is not contagious and is usually connected to seasonal allergies, irritation, or intolerance to medication or anything topical put on the face that comes in contact with your child's eyes.

Viral and bacterial conjunctivitis are contagious and usually occur from an upper respiratory tract infection, sore throat, or cold. These types require antibiotic drops or ointment from a doctor. A cold compress can also help relieve discomfort.

Nail Care

Your child is constantly playing and exploring, so it is not uncommon for her to get play dough, food, or dirt in her fingernails. **Try to keep her fingernails short so that they can collect the least amount of dirt.** Wash your child's hands frequently, especially after activities or outside time. You can use a nail brush or toothbrush to help clean under your toddler's fingernails.

Trimming

Trim your child's fingernails after a bath. Water softens the nails, making them easier to trim and cut. Sing a song or count her fingers to keep her engaged and patient while you finish.

Ear Care

At bath time, clean the outside crevices of your child's ear with a damp, soft cloth.

DO NOT probe the inside of the ear. The middle ear is not fully developed, and you could end up puncturing the eardrum.

Ear Infections

Ear infections are most common in the middle ear because the Eustachian tube, which is a small passage leading from the nose and mouth (connecting the esophagus) to the area of the middle ear, does not fully develop until age three. Because it is so small, the Eustachian tube gets clogged after a cold.

Signs that your child has an ear infection may be your child pulling on her ear or seeing drainage come from her ear. Go see your pediatrician. Ear infections can get painful.

Tooth Care

By the time she is three years old, your child will develop 20 primary teeth. By 15 months, your child's molars will start coming in. These can be extremely painful for your toddler. Offer your toddler teething toys or frozen fruits to gnaw on to soothe teething pains. Topical ointments for teething can numb gum areas inside the mouth. Consult your pediatrician before administering any medication orally.

Brushing Teeth

Try to get your child in the habit of brushing his teeth. Get a small-head toothbrush with soft, round bristles and brush your child's teeth in a circular motion along the sides and along the outer gum lines.

Brushing can help clean any food stuck in teeth and massage your child's gums while he is teething. **Let him brush his own teeth for a little while before you brush them.**

Teething and Biting

During the teething stage, toddlers also enter a biting stage. Children tend to bite because of a combination of teething and a lack of language skills. They are still learning to communicate what they want or need. Because toddlers are teething at this age, they are orally stimulated by the introduction to solid and crunchy foods. They begin to test the waters and see what will happen if they bite you or their friends.

Sometimes it is to see if they can bite through the skin and other times it is to see how the friend will react. Toddlers also tend to bite due to a lack of language skills that are necessary for them to express feelings like anger, frustration, joy, and excitement.

Toddlers turn to biting as a substitute message for "I am mad at you!" or "I am very excited!"

What can you do about biting?

* Have teething toys around for your toddler when he is teething so he has something else to bite.

* Build his language skills through sign language. Encourage him to use signs for words like *more*, *no*, and *up* so that he can communicate to you what he wants without getting frustrated.

* Mouth the words and say them slowly as you sign to help your toddler learn how to say the words as he signs them, too.

* Let your toddler know that teeth are for biting food and not friends. Redirect him to another activity so he can focus on something else.

Diet >
Calories, Allergies, Safety, and Tummy Troubles

Children (12 months to 24 months) need:

* 3 ounces of grains (one slice of bread or ½ cup of cooked rice or pasta),
* ½–1 cup of fruits (¾ cups juice, ½ cup canned fruit, ¼ cup dried fruit, 1 piece of fruit or melon wedge),
* ½ cup of vegetables (½ cup chopped raw or cooked vegetables, 1 cup raw leafy greens),
* 1–1 ½ cup cups of milk or other dairy products,
* 2 ounces of high-protein foods (meat, poultry, eggs, and legumes)—1 ounce meat, 1 egg, ¼ cup legumes such as beans, 2 tablespoons of peanut butter,
* 3–4 teaspoons of healthy oils such as canola oil, olive oil, or tub margarine,
* Fats and sweets are empty calories and should be avoided.

Calories

Your child needs about 1,000 calories a day to meet her growth, energy, and nutrition needs.

She has a small stomach and will need to eat every two and half to three hours. A typical eating schedule for a toddler is three meals and two snacks a day. The food groups that make up a balanced diet are proteins, carbohydrates, fruits, and dairy.

Allow your child to pick from a variety of healthful foods and vary the foods she eats because her tastes and preferences change frequently. Based on the activity level of a given day or an increase in her growth rate, her appetite may change as well.

Babies and toddlers should be getting at least half of their calories from fat. When they turn two and their rate of growth slows, gradually lower the percentage of calories from fat, eventually changing it to one-third of her daily calories when she reaches four or five years old.

Avoid adding too many flavors or spices to your toddler's food because she is still developing her taste buds and is more sensitive to flavorings than adults. Making foods that are too salty, spicy, sour, or sweet will prevent your child from experiencing the natural tastes of foods.

Cutting your child's food into bite-size pieces can also encourage her to start feeding herself. She can easily pick up her food and put it into her mouth.

Switching to Cow's Milk

At 12 months, your child is finally ready to switch to cow's milk.

It is important to wait until 12 months for your child to switch to cow's milk because of a variety of internal developments still happening in her body. At 12 months, your child now needs the calcium and vitamin D that whole milk supplies.

You should be giving your child whole milk until the age of two unless your physician tells you otherwise.

Only give your child between 16 and 20 ounces of milk a day; too much milk can affect her diet and make her too full to eat other meals and foods.

Trouble adjusting to whole milk?

* Mix cow's milk with your child's formula or breast milk so she can adjust to the taste.

* Try adding cow's milk to foods such as hot or cold cereal in the morning.

* If your child is really putting up a fight, try adding other calcium-rich foods to her diet, such as yogurts and cheeses.

Allergies

With the introduction of more varieties of food starting now and continuing throughout her life, your child can develop allergies.

Indications of allergies include sneezing, itching, swelling in the face, and skin rashes (small bumps).

Food allergies: Are usually quite rare and follow your child's genetic background. If you have a food allergy that runs in your family, be careful when giving your child that food. Food allergies in young children typically go away with age.

Hay fever:

Can happen with environmental or seasonal allergies when your child is allergic to pollen, grass, dust, or animal dander. Symptoms include watery eyes, sneezing, and a runny nose.

Because children this age cannot yet blow their noses to clear their nasal passages, mucus drips down their throats, causing them to cough.

Safety

Have your child sit at the table with you to eat so you can monitor her feeding herself to ensure that she does not put too much food in her mouth at one time. Keep adding to her plate as she finishes to encourage your child to take her time.

Because your toddler is teething, she may be very attracted to crunchy or hard foods at one point and then not like them later. Keep trying a variety of kid-friendly and safe foods; something she didn't like today can be her new favorite tomorrow. Let her choose what she wants to eat from the healthful choices you provide (e.g. a piece of fruit, carrot sticks, or wheat crackers with hummus) so that you are ultimately in charge of the choices.

Highchairs

What to look for in a highchair:

Safety:
* Does the highchair have buckles to secure your toddler?
* Does it have the JPMA (Juvenile Products Manufacturers Association) stamp of approval?
* Is it easy to get your child in and out of the highchair?

Comfort:
* Is the chair big enough for your your toddler?
* Is it comfortable for your toddler to sit through a whole meal?
* Is there a footrest to help with posture?
* What type of material is it made of? Is it easy to clean?

Sippy Cups

Most children at 12 months are ready to give up the bottle. Sippy cups have spouts that help your child switch from sucking to sipping, and they are mess free.

Things to look for in a sippy cup:

* no handles—this makes it easier to transition to a cup later;
* removable top—for easy cleaning;
* weighted bottom—some sippy cups come with a weighted bottom, which is a great way to control messy leaks;
* types of plastic—stay away from any plastic cups or utensils that contain BPA or say Recycle 7 or have the letters PC on the product. These are not safe for your young one.

Tummy Troubles

Constipation

Constipation is not always a sign of illness but can make your child uncomfortable. Constipation is usually accompanied by hard or painful stools.

What to do:

* Increase fluids: Give your child more water to drink.
* Diet: Make sure you are giving your child correct portion sizes when it comes to food and also change the variety of foods you offer. Introduce more fruits and vegetables.
* Try prunes, dried fruits (raisins and apricots), oatmeal, or green vegetables.
* Stay away from cow's milk, yogurt, cheese, cooked carrots, and bananas.

Diarrhea

Diarrhea is the opposite of constipation and involves very loose or too many bowel movements. Diarrhea can cause your child pain as well as make him become dehydrated and lethargic. Diarrhea can be caused by a virus or contaminated food or can be a side effect of medication.

If diarrhea starts quickly but ends by the next meal your child eats and isn't accompanied by fever, you probably should not be concerned.

Avoid:

* Drinks with sugar like soda or ginger ale; sugar may upset the stomach.

Vomiting

Vomiting is a virus caused by bacteria or a parasite. It can sometimes be followed by diarrhea.

Signs your child may be dehydrated include:

* not urinating,
* dry lips and mouth,
* looks pale.

What to do:

If your child is having trouble holding down liquids or food, try to rehydrate her with an oral rehydration solution.

Examples of oral rehydration solutions include:

* water,
* Pedialyte®,
* watered-down juice,
* chicken broth.

When administering oral rehydration solutions:

1. Give your child only a teaspoon of fluid every five minutes to help her keep it down.
2. If your child is able to keep the liquid down, keep increasing the amount of fluid you give her.
3. Keep giving your child fluids until your child stops vomiting.
4. If your child is ready to eat again, try to stick to these foods:

* dry toast,
* small amount of pasta (no sauce),
* hard-boiled egg,
* rice,
* bananas.

Potty Training >
Are We Ready?

Eighteen months to three years old is the average age to show interest in and start trying to potty train.

Signs your child may be ready for potty training:

* begins to communicate having a dirty diaper—your child may verbally tell you or draw your attention to her diaper by patting it or pointing to it;
* begins to show discomfort when wet or soiled—your child may walk with a wide stride or begin to pull and take off her soiled diaper;
* shows interest in the potty—models potty training with toys, dolls, or even herself;
* displays independence—starts to pull her pants on and off and follows basic one- and two-step directions.

Regularity
* is able to stay dry for up to two hours between diaper changes—shows that the bladder is maturing, and she is able to hold it longer;
* starts to have regular bowel movements at the same time every day.

Ready to Start?

* Stay close to home.
* Try no underpants or underwear.
* Try to encourage the most tries as possible so your child can get used to the feeling of going.
* Give your child plenty of salty snacks that make her thirsty. Diluting juice to drink will encourage peeing and support potty training quickly.
* Have all materials present at the potty (toilet paper, underwear or pullup, change of clothing if necessary).
* **Let her bring her favorite toy or stuffed animal to model potty training.**

Verbal Praise:

Be excited about your child using the potty!

* Sing a song, do a dance, clap your hands, and tell her with a smile you are proud of her.
* Don't be upset or annoyed when she has an accident. Remind her that pee goes in the potty. Have her help you clean up, do laundry, or get clean clothes together.

Follow Through

Potty on the go:

Invest in a travel potty to encourage consistency. It is important to keep up with your routine even when at Grandma's house, with your babysitter, or at school.

* The more days you get into potty training, the more consistent your child's potty times will become. Having a routine with nap and eating times adds to consistency.
* Have all your materials with you, such as wipes, clean underwear, and plastic bags for soiled clothes.

Potty time doesn't mean missing play time!

Don't make your child feel like going potty means she is missing out on an activity.

* Move the potty to the activity. If everyone is outside, let your child use the potty while she is outside so she doesn't put up a fight.
* Encourage your child to try before you start an activity or before you go somewhere. Have her try before and after lunch, as well as before you start a game or put out a new set of toys.

Routine >
Two Naps to One

Napping is important for your toddler and for you. She needs an opportunity to refuel her body with energy; otherwise, everyone in the house will feel the effects.

It is important to stay attuned to your child's cues for needing a nap. You may notice her staring into space, rubbing her eyes, or crying to signal it is time. Usually around 12 months, you will notice changes in your child's sleep schedule. Before turning 12 months old, most infants are on a two-nap schedule. Seventeen percent of children have already transitioned to a one-nap schedule by 12 months. At around 15 or 16 months, almost 60% of children have fully transitioned to a one-nap schedule.

It is common for children to change nap schedules from time to time. If your child has been showing you these signs, then it could be time for a change:

* crying or fighting nap times,
* waking up tired after too short a nap,
* not taking a nap at all,
* waking up in the middle of the night.

What is the best way to transition from two naps to one? Like many milestones in your child's life, moving from two naps to one is a gradual process that takes routine and consistency.

It can take anywhere from a few weeks to a few months for your child to transition to a one-nap schedule.

Put your child in the same place for nap each day. Don't let her nap in the stroller one day and in your bed the next. It is important for the nap place and environment to be consistent so your child will develop a routine for sleeping.

If your child wakes up early from her one afternoon nap, try soothing her back to sleep and see if she will sleep longer. Play some music or pat her back to see if she will fall back asleep.

One nap does not mean less sleep. Most toddlers need between 12 and 14 hours of sleep a day until they reach the age of three.

> **Tips for a smooth transition:**
>
> **Adjusting your child's schedule**
> Try pushing his morning nap back by 15 minutes every day or two. You can also try to decrease the morning nap by 15 minutes every few days to shorten your child's morning rest and better preserve the afternoon naptime.
>
> **Winding down**
> Try finding activities that are calm and help your child relax before she goes down for a nap. Establish a naptime routine of reading a book or listening to calming music. Sound machines offer soothing sounds such as beach waves or rain falling that can help signal naptime.
>
> **Things to keep in mind**
> Many children are fine with one-nap schedules during the week but vary on the weekends. Try to be as consistent as possible on the weekends, but let your child take an extra nap if needed.

Mind and Body >

Aggressive Behavior

It is not uncommon for little ones to engage in some aggressive behavior, such as hitting and biting. Aggressive behavior is their form of communicating when they are frustrated because they have not yet learned the words to express their feelings; however, if your child is exhibiting numerous aggressive behaviors every day, he may need some help from you.

There are many ways to deal with aggressive behavior in a child. Before getting frustrated with your child's aggressive behaviors, try to observe when these behaviors happen. Look for patterns such as where, when, with whom, and what time the aggressive behaviors happen most.

If they happen around the same time every day, your toddler may be tired or hungry. Try to adjust his schedule.

If the aggressive behavior happens more often in public places than at home, think about the possible stimulation and who is around. Your child may be having a hard time getting your attention or feel a lack of control if he is in a place with which he is not familiar.

Always look at outside factors as well. Changes in routine or in the family can cause your child to act out for attention or out of frustration.

It is important to let your caregivers know if there are any changes at home and to make activities and routines as normal as possible.

Lastly, think of your child's temperament. Each child is different and has a different comfort level. Some children have a hard time meeting new people; others have difficulty communicating. Brainstorm ways to help your child, such as communicating through sign language or talking about an event before it occurs.

Yoga

Having your toddler participate in yoga can help an aggressive child funnel that energy into physical movement. Better still, yoga gives her the ability to exercise both her body and mind. Yoga encompasses the whole child by both strengthening children's bodies and calming their minds to better shape focus and build self-confidence. Through yoga, children are able to develop and foster more than just physical skills.

Yoga helps your toddler develop social-emotional skills such as self-regulation. Yoga is a great tool to help your child redirect her energy and emotions and better calm herself.

Physically, your toddler is learning how to manipulate her body and better maximize her mobility. She is exploring different ways of using her muscles to pull herself up, climb, and move from place to place.

Yoga is a great tool to build creativity and imagination. Your child can express herself through different movements. As a parent, you can incorporate different music, relatable animal or nature poses, and dance. Remember: Healthful habits started young will help with developmental successes as she grows.

Remember, the Whole Child Parenting Program offers appropriate developmental products and monthly activity books that walk you through supporting your child's skills. Using these in conjunction with the recommended age-appropriate room materials ensures faster development.

Reaching Milestones >

As your child continues to grow and mature you will see that she is unique. Growth and developmental stages are sequential, variable, and individual. The stages can occur in the same order as other children and the differences in how long the stages last will vary from child to child. You are an important component to the success of your child's development. Providing a caring and loving home and spending time with your toddler—playing, singing, reading books, and even just talking—will put her on the path to success!

The information below is a guide to explain some of the developmental milestones an average toddler will achieve. These skills may not all occur between the 13–24-month period; skills can develop within a six-month to a year range. Consider what you read in the context of your child's unique development.

COGNITIVE

- Builds a tower of at least 2–3 blocks and then knocks them over. Around 18 months can build a tower of 3 blocks, perhaps independently.
- Learns to explore objects and toys in a more complex way. Can organize toys, e.g. putting all the blocks the same color in a spot.
- Might be restless, but is able to sustain attention to one structured activity for 2–3 minutes; external noises and distractions may hamper this.
- Knows objects are used for specific purposes, e.g. using a toy key to put in a door.
- Will be able to complete simple chunky puzzles (ones with knobs will be easier to hold) of 2–4 pieces.

SOCIAL-EMOTIONAL

- Wants to be more independent and do things without your help.
- Can recognize distress in others (like when she sees a friend cry)—beginning of empathy.
- Gets frustrated trying to express herself. It is a time your toddler will need you to listen patiently and put into words what you think she is trying to say. This will help your child feel understood.
- She is learning how to care for others by the way you care for her. She may rub your back or comfort you when you look sad.
- Likes to play alone. Is emotionally attached to her toys or objects for security reasons.

TODDLER > REACHING MILESTONES

LANGUAGE

- By the end of the toddler years, will say at least 35 words on her own—without imitating you.
- Understands and responds to words or questions such as, "Do you want water?"
- Shows desires by pointing or using vocalization of words.
- Loves to hear and read stories with you, especially about things she knows: animals, families, and other toddlers that look like her.
- Will use social words (*bye-bye*); requesting words (*more*); early pronouns (such as *me*, *mine*); location words (*up*, *down*); adjectives and adverbs (*yucky*, *fast*).

CREATIVE

- Begins to pretend and imitate in play.
- Shakes bells, likes songs, finger plays like "Itsy Bitsy Spider" and rhymes with nonsense words.
- Scribbles with crayons, finger paints on paper, makes crayon dots on paper.
- Uses fingers to swirl finger paint or shaving cream, squeezes oily molding dough.
- Holds and pats a baby doll, sits stuffed animals at a table.

PHYSICAL

- Walks with feet slightly apart.
- Climbs. Is beginning to manage corners and obstacles better. Curiosity will lead to her to explore "off-limit" territories. You will need to take extra steps to keep your child safe and help her learn right from wrong.
- Climbs up stairs with support from others in her environment.
- Holds a crayon with a fist grip and scribbles using preferred hand.
- Can hold a cup and use a spoon to eat.

HEALTH AND CARE

- Drinks from a cup, picks up finger food, and feeds self with spoon.
- Puts clothes in a hamper if asked and directed.
- Washes hands with help.
- Attempts to put on shoes, socks, and jacket.

Environment >
Toddler's Room

When you give your toddler toys and furnish her room you are supporting learning in a natural environment: your home.

It is the place where she will learn to master all **six areas of development: cognitive, social-emotional, language, creative, physical, and health.**

It might look like just child's play, but your toddler is hard at work learning important skills. Each new skill lets her progress to the next one, building on a foundation that leads to more complicated tasks.

In order for all of this to occur your toddler needs just the right learning environment.

There are several steps you will take to set up your home for learning. First you eliminate items in your child's room that make it look and feel cluttered.

Then you create a space in which your child feels free to make messes and play with few restrictions. You begin to achieve mindful organization by placing all skill-developing materials in your **Six Drawer Whole Child Color-Coded Organizer**.

The following picture shows what the recommended toddler room looks like. Many of the activities you will do with your toddler will occur in this space, an environment filled with furniture that has a purpose and age-appropriate toys.

Whole Child: Toddler's Room

The following list contains must-have items for your toddler's room. These items will be used interchangeably with your other Whole Child Parenting materials.

1. Six Drawer Whole Child Color-Coded Organizer
2. Whole Child Wall Planner
3. Table and Chairs
4. Easel
5. Carpet
6. Bookshelf
7. Step Climber
8. Kitchen Set
9. Puppet/Pretend Play Materials

1. Six Drawer Whole Child Color-Coded Organizer
Easily organize educational materials and toys by six areas of development. Ensure your child always has enough materials in each drawer.

2. Whole Child Wall Planner
Plan and organize weekly activities based on six areas of development.

3. Table and Chairs
Provides a clearly defined space, at child's level and shaped to support posture, for child to work independently and stay focused. Use for fine motor development and learning shapes, colors, spatial concepts, science, letters, and numbers.

4. Easel
Provides a place for child to play with well-organized art materials displayed at eye level. Materials are easily changed out by child with help or by parent. Use for fostering development of child's aesthetic sense and for engaging in creative experiences.

5. Carpet
Provides a soft, safe place, free from clutter, for your child to play on. Use for providing materials in one central location at child's eye level. Enables parent to change out materials and still maintain child safety.

6. Bookshelf
Makes books easily accessible to child and supports independent exploration and literacy skills. Use for bonding with child through one-on-one time.

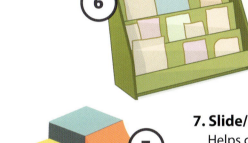

7. Slide/Step Climber
Helps child develop physical skills by allowing freedom of movement, with open pathways for crawling, low steps to climb, surfaces with different textures, tunnel, and slide.

8. Kitchen Set
Organize props and pretend food. Can be easily rotated in and out. Use to develop self-help skills, independence, and imagination.

9. Puppet/Pretend Play Materials
Helps social communication, and interactive skills through shared experiences. Use for pretend play and peek-a-boo games.

whole child activity books >

Have a look at a sample of our series of activity books for toddlers. This series of 6 titles helps toddlers exercise their brains and bodies in every category of development explored in the Whole Child Parenting books. The 6 titles are available now.

WHOLE CHILD Activity Book

Toddler (12 to 24 Months)

Transportation

WHOLE CHILD = (smart + creative) / (healthy + happy)

COGNITIVE DEVELOPMENT
Problem-solving • Attention • Numbers

SOCIAL-EMOTIONAL DEVELOPMENT
Self-control • Friendship • Feelings

LANGUAGE DEVELOPMENT
Communication • Speaking • Literacy

CREATIVE DEVELOPMENT
Dramatic Play • Dance • Music • Arts

PHYSICAL DEVELOPMENT
Motor Skills: Sensory, Gross, Fine

HEALTH AND CARE
Hygiene • Diet • Routine • Yoga

sneak peek >

1

EARLY MATH SKILLS

DISCOVER!
You will see your child developing cognitive skills such as learning opposites like *big* and *small*. Your child will spend much of her time exploring the physical aspects of these concepts by placing objects next to each other and seeing the relationships between the objects.

DID YOU KNOW?
One of the easiest ways you can build your toddler's cognitive skills is through rhyming and simple games like I Spy, in which together you look for items that are *big* or *small* in your environment.

LET'S DO MORE!
Have your child use two hands to pick up a big train, but only one hand to pick up a small one.

BIG AND SMALL

Skill • Learning spatial concepts

Directions: With your child look at the trains below. Ask your child to point to the *big* train (give cue by pointing). Have your child color the train using a purple crayon. Next ask your child to point to the *small* train (give cue by pointing). Praise your child, "Good job coloring!"

Understanding the concepts big and small will help your toddler build the foundation needed for learning more about sizes and simple math concepts.

sneak peek >

2

EMOTIONAL DEVELOPMENT

DISCOVER!
Sign language encourages your child to interact with others by moving his hands to make signs for words. Sign language is a great tool that can benefit him both socially and emotionally as he learns new ways to express his thoughts and feelings.

DID YOU KNOW?
Signing helps eliminate the frustration your child feels when he can't communicate. Even toddlers can learn to use manners when signing. Though he does not yet understand the importance of the social graciousness of these words, he can include that *please* and *thank you* to help him get what he wants.

LET'S DO MORE!
Each time you are going to do an activity that involves your car, say the word and make the sign for *car* before getting in and out. To sign the word *car*, hold your hands in fists in front of you as if you are gripping a steering wheel. Then move your hands up and down in a circle as if you are driving.

SIGN LANGUAGE

Skill • Learning to sign

Directions: With your child point to and look at the picture of the sign for *sleep* in the box. Say the word out loud while showing your child the sign. Have your child imitate you and perform the sign.

To sign *sleep*, start with fingers extended and spread apart. Beginning with your hand over your face, move your fingers down to end with your hand below your chin and your fingers touching your thumb. As you make the sign, relax your face and close your eyes to add to the sleepy effect.

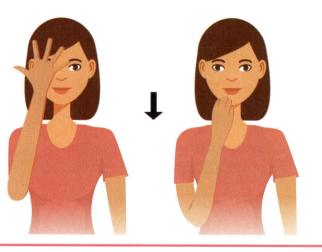

Using sign language to communicate with your toddler helps his self-regulation skills. For example, he may not be able to tell you verbally he is tired, but he will be able to express it by showing you the sign.

sneak peek >

whole child parenting program >

Get a sneak peek into the next Whole Child Parenting book. ***Whole Child Parenting: Age Two*** is a comprehensive look into the development of children ages 24–36 months. The book is available now.

WHOLE CHILD
PARENTING

AGE TWO

Parents, educators, and caregivers will learn how best to encourage growth and skill-building in all six developmental areas.

sneak peek >

Milestones for a Two Year Old

COGNITIVE — 1
- Can do simple sorting
- Recognizes and names colors
- Sings parts of simple songs
- Recalls past experiences

SOCIAL-EMOTIONAL — 2
- Shows independence and awareness of body parts
- Identifies and talks about personal feelings
- Shows interest in helping with basic tasks

LANGUAGE — 3
- Shows interest in books
- Puts together simple sentences
- Can talk about books
- Can tell own age
- Knows first and last name

CREATIVE — 4
- Believes stuffed animals are friends
- Plays with rhyming words
- Moves to music

PHYSICAL — 5
- Runs with ease
- Bends over easily
- Rides a tricycle
- Holds markers and crayons

HEALTH AND CARE — 6
- Almost all teeth in place
- Controls motor behaviors
- Body looks more proportional, longer legs and arms
- Potty trains, able to stay dry between potty times

TWO YEAR OLD > MILESTONES   3

two

Two year olds are thirsty for knowledge and are constantly exploring their environment and asking the question "Why?" They are starting to problem solve on their own, make connections, and categorize things based on color, shape, and size. This is an exciting time for your child in which you can introduce them to new languages, skills, and environments. Let's look at these milestones and more in the six areas of a two year old's development.

sneak peek >

1. Cognitive Development

> **Cognitive development refers to how your child's mind is working and his process of learning.**

At two years old, your child's brain grows so fast that 250,000 nerve cells are added every minute. Your child's brain continues to grow after birth; by two years of age, your child's brain will be about 80% of the size of an adult brain.

In this year, your child's learning process is becoming more thoughtful and is greatly influenced by his environment. Your child is naturally curious and inquisitive and through his play investigates to make sense of the world around him.

During this stage of development, two year olds demonstrate how their minds are making more connections. Your child is moving past just observing and manipulating objects in his environment and is now beginning to understand the relationship between objects and ideas.

The following chart provides you with an image that walks you through the stages of your child's intellectual development.

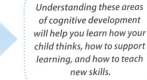

Understanding these areas of cognitive development will help you learn how your child thinks, how to support learning, and how to teach new skills.

TWO YEAR OLD > COGNITIVE DEVELOPMENT   5

Whole Child: age two
Cognitive Development Components

Under each cognitive area, the chart below gives you specific skills you can expect to see as your two year old develops. This chart will allow you to have practical expectations for your child at this age.

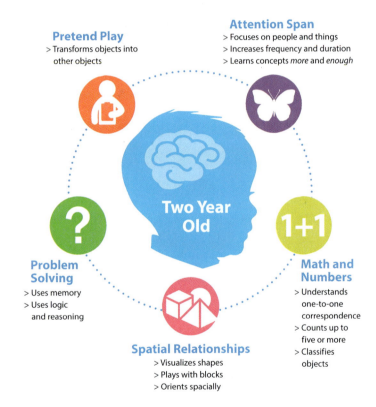

Pretend Play
> Transforms objects into other objects

Attention Span
> Focuses on people and things
> Increases frequency and duration
> Learns concepts *more* and *enough*

Problem Solving
> Uses memory
> Uses logic and reasoning

Spatial Relationships
> Visualizes shapes
> Plays with blocks
> Orients spacially

Math and Numbers
> Understands one-to-one correspondence
> Counts up to five or more
> Classifies objects

TWO YEAR OLD > COGNITIVE DEVELOPMENT   7

Through his senses and developing motor skills, your child will use cause and effect and reasoning to explore unfamiliar objects. You will see your child start making connections between items and then begin organizing them into groups and categories.

Some of these connections can be seen through simple tasks such as sorting toys by color as well as through symbolic play, in which your child may use one object to represent another based on its physical features such as shape or size.

As parents, it is important to provide everyday activities that tap into your child's curiosity to help nourish the brain, which, in turn, will increase your child's learning efficiency and brain capacity. Any mental stimulation provided to your child will activate his mind and protect against cognitive decline.

You are preparing your child for the Olympics, and you have about four years to do it. This will feel like a lot of time, but in actuality, four years will go by very quickly. Similar to the training of an athlete in the Olympics, the brain gets activated (warms up) and develops (refines skills) through repeated experience (workouts), interactions (team play), and environmental exposure (proper equipment and practice area), leading to greater performance.

Your child's brain is preparing for the Olympics as well, and in this case, the first four years are the most crucial for starting on the right path to developing your child's full potential.

The subsequent chapters show you how your child acquires knowledge and demonstrates major development in brain growth.

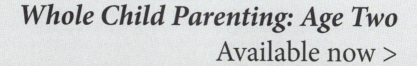

Whole Child Parenting: Age Two
Available now >

WHOLE CHILD

Parenting Program books and materials are available worldwide.

Also available separately

Birth to Age Five

The book that kick started the program!

INFANT
(Birth to 12 Months)

TODDLER
(12 to 24 Months)

AGE TWO

AGE THREE

AGE FOUR

Whole Child Program Activity Books

- 4 **Infant** Titles
- 6 **Toddler** Titles
- 12 **Age Two** Titles
- 12 **Age Three** Titles
- 12 **Age Four** Titles

Whole Child Program books and materials are available at special discounts when purchased in bulk for premiums and sales promotions as well as for fundraising or educational use. For details, please contact us at: sales@wholechild.co

Visit us on the web at: www.wholechild.co